WORKING THE ROOM:
NETWORKING FOR PROFESSIONALS
2nd Edition

by
Stevie Ray

Punchline
Publications

Copyright © 2009 Stephen M. Rentfrow
2nd Edition, 2017
All rights reserved.
Printed in the United States of America.

No part of this book may be used or reproduced in any manner whatsoever without the written permission of the publisher except that portions may be used in broadcast or printed commentary or review when attributed fully to the author and publication by name.
For information address:

Punchline Publications
10700 Cambridge Ct.
Burnsville, MN 55337

Cover design by:
Dragan Bilic
Vrsac, Serbia

Punchline Publications is a division of
Stevie Ray's Improv Company
Contact at:
www.stevierays.org

"Making it up as we go since 1989"

This book is dedicated to:

Everyone who has ever scanned a roomful of people at a networking function and thought, "Thank God there is a bar."

Acknowledgement:

Pamela Mayne, business partner and great friend. We founded Stevie Ray's Improv Company in 1989 and have been *making it up as we go* since then.

Gary Jader, former member of the Board of Directors of Stevie Ray's Improv Company. Many of the concepts and exercises in this book were developed in collaboration with Gary. Except the good ideas are mine.

Thanks to:

Kanitta, my lovely wife. Kanitta and I met at a business function in 1996 and knew that there was a spark, but business etiquette kept us from pursuing anything more than a friendship. After no contact for twelve years, I sat in my house one day thinking, "She was the one that got away." I sent a letter (remember those things with paper and envelopes?) to her last known address. We reconnected and were married two years later. How's that for great networking?

Ondine, my stepdaughter. You taught me as much about networking as any business mentor. Someday you will admit that my jokes really are funny.

Contents

Introduction ... 1

PART I
Learn to Love Networking ... 5

1. Marketing Yourself ... 13
2. The Real Opportunities ... 51
3. Do This, Don't Do That ... 61

PART II
Working the Room ... 83

4. "So, What Do You Do?" ... 89
5. Get Out of the Prom Circle ... 107
6. Now What Do I Say? ... 117
7. Common Questions ... 123
8. Making It Work ... 163

A Final Word ... 167

WORKING THE ROOM:
NETWORKING FOR PROFESSIONALS
2nd Edition

Introduction

I was talking to a small group of people just before a chamber of commerce meeting when the subject of networking came up. Some in the group grumbled about how networking events feel so phony, or about how networking never seems to produce anything. However, one woman blurted out, "I love networking! Love it, love it, love it. Just give me a roomful of people and a handful of business cards and I'm good to go."

Later, I watched her work the room. She flitted from group to group with big smile and firm handshake, "Hi, Susie Jamison with Jamison and Associates. Here take my card." "Hi, Susie Jamison with Jamison and Associates. Have a business card." During each five-second interaction, she shoved her business card into the hand of her new "best friend." Her energy level was ten out of ten, but her sincerity was a level two at best. She left the event thinking that she had done her job. After all, she had gotten her business card into everyone's hand. Isn't that what networking is all about? All she had to do now was sit back and wait for the phone to ring.

You might expect that Susie's business cards were immediately dumped in the trash as soon as she was out of sight, but you would be wrong. People were so turned off by her that they didn't even wait to find a trash can. Her business cards made a lovely mosaic pattern on the carpet as they were scattered across the floor. But hey, she met everyone and shook their hands, so she had networked, right?

I was the speaker at another association meeting, and I stuck around to observe the networking session that followed. As a trainer, it is important to observe people in action. Just like a National Geographic photographer hiding behind bushes in the Serengeti to observe a pack of lions, I pick a spot to watch strange creatures called *humans* engage in the ritualistic dance called "networking." If you think modern humans have advanced beyond our days of dancing around a fire after dinner, observe a networking session. We haven't.

During that session, I observed a double-team version of Susie's approach. A husband-and-wife couple who owned a business together roamed the room with fliers in their hands. They had divided the room between then, like lions dividing a herd to single out easy prey. He attacked one half, and she attacked the other. Their mission — get those "Half-Off Sale" fliers into everyone's hands. They would each descend upon pairs, small groups, or someone standing alone at the bar. They would interrupt whatever conversation was taking place, slip the flier into everyone's hands with, "We've got a great special going on. Hope to see you there," and then dash off to the next victim.

After a while, the room became keenly aware, and wary, of the couple. When people saw either of them approaching, they positioned themselves in their groups such that someone else would bear the brunt of the attack. It was just like putting the weakest of the herd out as bait to protect the rest. The couple left having distributed all of their fliers; except a small pile, which they left at the front table. To be honest, the fliers did come in handy. People used the back side to write notes about conversations they had with people they actually did want to meet again. The stack at the front table went home with the server who was cleaning up. "I use these for my kid's drawing projects," he told me.

There is an old rule in business; don't advertise your product unless you know it is valuable. If you advertise a poor product, you only ensure that more people will discover how bad it is, and even more people will avoid your business. Businesses have many ways to make sure their product is perfect before opening their doors. Restaurants will have pre-opening nights so the staff can practice delivering the best service. Theatres will have preview performances to work out any glitches in the show before opening night. However, most people approach networking by saying to themselves, "Next time, I'll do better." Imagine a surgeon who plans to practice on the next patient. With networking, it pays to sharpen your skills before you have your grand opening.

PART I

Learn to Love Networking

I have to confess, the guy writing this book isn't any more thrilled about networking than you are. Most people don't; but, like me, they do enjoy meeting friends and having a relaxed, casual conversation. The reason we hate networking is that conversations during networking are rarely relaxed nor casual.

First, let's agree on a rule: there is a clear difference between networking and socializing. Networking is any time you have an opportunity to make a connection that could mean business; whether at a formal business function, or a chance encounter on a plane. Socializing is conversation with no agenda attached. Socializing may lead to networking, and vice versa, but they are not the same. And if you want to increase your business, you must first keep a clear distinction between the two. I have certainly been guilty of returning from a networking function only to realize that, while I had some great conversations, I didn't make one contact that could improve my business. Perhaps my discomfort with networking caused me to focus on socializing. Ever happen to you?

There is an obvious reason most people don't like networking. It is because, no matter what the other person is saying, we know there is an agenda to the conversation. Hidden agendas cause immediate distrust. A used car salesman can't even comment on the nice weather without us thinking that he is setting us up for a con job later in the conversation. It is actually a surprising relief when people are upfront with their intentions, "I am looking to partner with a business that…" This type of honesty only works, however, if the relationship being proposed is mutually beneficial. The husband-wife team running around the room handing out discount coupons did not have a mutually beneficial proposal.

Another, more visceral, reason we are uncomfortable with networking is that the human brain is wired to desire a certain kind of communication, and business conversations are not a natural fit for that three pound organ on top of our shoulders. We have evolved as a social creature, so you would think interacting with others would be a snap, but we evolved communicating within small social groups; a nuclear family along with a tribe of friends. Over eons of evolution, the brain has come to expect that arrangement. The brain simply isn't wired to encounter large numbers of strangers. In fact, neurologists and psychologists generally note that the brain can handle about thirty other brains in its sphere of acquaintances; any more brains than thirty causes a shut-down. This is why having small departments within large companies is a good thing, it provides a less stressful environment for the brain to do the work we ask of it.

This is why living in crowded cities carries a high degree of stress; too many unknown humans. To manage this stress, it is common for city dwellers to develop a mechanism of shutting out most of the people they encounter. Look at a crowded subway car and you will see very little eye contact, and body language that puts invisible walls between people.

The brain also has a default mechanism that is constantly running any time we are conscious. That default drive is the *safety* mechanism. In order for a weak species like humans to survive, the brain developed a keen ability to sense danger. In fact, avoiding danger is more important to the brain than seeking a positive experience. For instance, finding a bush full of berries to eat is certainly a positive experience, but not nearly as important as avoiding the bear that wants those berries, too. As such, evolution has left us with a brain that is primarily concerned with avoiding danger. For the entire time we are conscious, the brain is looking out for danger; real or perceived. Quite often, if the brain can't find danger, it will create it. This is why some people over-stress about events that aren't that important.

When it comes to meeting new people, this danger-sensing mechanism is in full force. Every new person we meet is quickly assessed and given a grade of *safe* or *not safe*. Psychologists call this the *Approach/Withdraw Response*. When we encounter someone new, the Limbic system—the brain's more instinctive functions that control base emotions—immediately gives them the once-over. If we get a positive feeling about the person, the Approach Response is engaged. We believe what the person says, we trust him or her, and we try to spend more time in their company. However, if we get a negative feeling, the Withdraw Response is activated and we distrust the person, we don't believe what they say, and we look for ways to distance ourselves from them. When the Withdraw Response is in effect, we may find ourselves disagreeing with the person, even if they say something that we would ordinarily agree with.

The Approach/Withdraw Response, being part of the reactive, limbic system, is a subconscious response; and it can be over-ridden by conscious thought. This can be a good thing, or bad, depending on the circumstance. The Approach/Withdraw Response is what we call a *gut reaction*, and we have all either listened to our gut, or talked ourselves into ignoring it. Remember the time you met someone you found attractive? You felt a strong pull to this person, but there was a little voice in your head telling you there was something wrong with the person. You didn't know why you felt the instinct to turn away, so you talked yourself out of listening to your gut; and you dated him anyway. Six months later, as you sat with friends talking about what a loser he turned out to be, you said "I knew there was something wrong with that guy." The gut is usually right.

I say "usually" because the gut isn't *always* right. Remember that the brain is always looking for danger. And, like anyone who has a job and wants to justify having the job, the brain will justify its mission by creating fear when fear is not warranted. In a fascinating experiment, test subjects were placed in a viewing booth which flashed photos of people's faces. A monitor was attached to the subject to provide a read-out of the person's blood chemicals. Whenever a face was displayed that was from a different geographical region than the subject, the subject's auto-immune levels in the blood spiked.

This may sound surprising. After all, the auto-immune system is a subconscious mechanism in the body to protect us from disease. But, if you think back through history, humans have always been at risk of dying from the germs and pathogens carried by people from unknown regions. In fact, more people have died throughout history from germs than from guns or spears. So the brain has developed a secret response, whenever it sees a face that is from somewhere unknown, it kicks the auto-immune system into high gear. When the researchers showed a photo, and then followed it up with a tape of the person speaking, if the voice had a foreign dialect the auto-immune system spiked again. The face and the voice were all it took for the brain to recognize danger.

Perhaps this is why racism is an automatic response for humans. When we see or hear a stranger, the brain senses danger. However, this is an opportunity for the higher brain to take over; to talk yourself out of a gut reaction that is not necessarily accurate. Once you start conversing with a stranger, and the more commonalities you discover, you realize that the gut reaction of fear was simply a hold-over from a time when strangers always meant danger.

If you cause a Withdraw Response in someone else, you can turn it around and still create a good connection, but it will take a lot more work; and the result is far from guaranteed. So you need to make a good connection, and fast. We have all heard advice about how long it takes to make a good impression; from a few seconds to the traditional *Thirty Second Rule*. In reality, there are so many different functions going on in the brain during a personal encounter that there are different milestones for making a good impression.

First, the Approach/Withdraw Response happens in a matter of milliseconds. This is because the visual cortex of the brain evolved before the auditory cortex. The visual cortex is much larger and more efficient at evaluating input than the auditory cortex. We obviously see someone before we hear them, so the visual cortex has the first crack at judging them. Nice posture? Commanding presence without being over-bearing? Good smile? Nicely attired? All of these reach the visual cortex in less than a second. Then the voice jumps into the picture. Is the volume appropriate for the room (not "Is the voice loud or soft?" but is it the right volume for the situation?). Is the tone confident? However, as important as the auditory signals are, because the visual cortex holds more influence over decision making, what you say will never be as important as what I see. After this initial subconscious reaction, psychologists say that a full-seated impression of someone takes about twenty seconds to register. Not much time, so let's make sure you are making the most of it.

With all this pressure to get networking just right, why even do it? Wouldn't it be better to simply create a list of connections online and market yourself to them? As much as going to another networking event, or striking up a conversation with a stranger at a conference might seem stressful, it is still the best way to earn business. Corporate leaders, HR directors, and recruiters all report that online services are only marginally effective; and they only provide an introduction. Business is still won or lost face to face. There is no way that electronic medium can replace the power of human interaction.

Organizations that sponsor networking events—chambers of commerce, professional associations, rodeo clown parties—have long recognized the frustration of those who attend. These organizations try to improve the outcome by "managing" the process. They try structured networking activities that bear a striking resemblance to speed dating. Few people find their spouses at speed dating events, and few people find good business prospects by networking the same way.

The challenge of networking is the same as speed-dating, if you don't develop the right skills before you meet someone, it doesn't matter how structured the approach is, you are still advertising a lousy product. That is why this book contains exercises for you to practice. I know, people hate practicing. Frankly, so do I. If I loved to practice, I would have been first chair trombone in junior high school.

Don't look at these exercises as work; look upon them as games you can play every now and then. And I mean *play*. Have an attitude of fun, the way people would like to see you when they network with you.

Some of the games take a bit of setting up in order to play; if you don't have that opportunity you can easily adjust them to include them in your everyday activities. Just make sure you play them regularly. Professional athletes don't hit the field without working on the fundamentals. Musicians don't walk into a concert without practicing scales. These exercises are meant to be your dribbling practice or your musical scales.

CHAPTER 1

Marketing Yourself

Gary Jader, mentioned in the acknowledgments, is a marketing professional. He refers to networking as, *The Not-So-Subtle Art of Marketing You*. If you look at the true nature of marketing, he is right. Every commercial on TV or radio is meant to get you to trust the person doing the selling, and to go beyond a mild interest in the product to become excited about it. Commercials don't sell products by simply stating their qualities and hoping you will buy them. However, people often try to sell themselves that way, listing off their qualifications and hoping that will do the trick. There are a number of psychological factors at play when people are deciding whether to work with you.

Emotion vs. Fact

One basic principle of marketing that applies to networking is that *People buy with emotion and justify with fact*. Look around your house. Most of the things you own you probably bought on impulse. Grocery store owners estimate that over 50% of purchases made in their stores are impulse buys. Look at how many people own Sport Utility Vehicles. When you compare the facts, SUV's are actually a poorer choice of vehicle than many other options. A minivan is better at ferrying people and carrying cargo. Yet minivans lose the battle of emotional pull. SUV owners are cool, minivan owners are "Soccer Moms."

People buy based on an emotional connection to the product, but they don't justify their decision using emotions. A man will buy a big, huge, four-wheel drive truck because he sees a TV commercial showing another guy driving the truck up a mountain of rocks. The man thinks, "I have to get that truck!" Forget the fact that he is an accountant living in urbanville with not a mountain of rock in sight. All he has to put in the bed of the truck is a briefcase. Emotion overcomes intellect every time. When you ask him why he bought the truck, he will never cite emotion ("I bought this truck to satisfy my feelings of inadequacy.") To justify a choice, we rely on reason; "It has a great warranty, gets good gas mileage…" If we are emotionally connected to something, we will create any reason we can to justify the purchase.

When the former professional wrestler, Jesse Ventura, became governor of my home state of Minnesota, one of the initiatives he fought for was the introduction of light-rail transit for Minneapolis and St. Paul. It was a long battle for him to get light right accepted by other politicians and the public. The state was doubtful that such a venture would be successful. People who were against the idea presented the arguments, "Our population is too spread out to make it useful." "We're too accustomed to driving where we want to go, we won't want the inconvenience." "The project won't make enough money and will need government subsidy to survive." and "Buses can go anywhere, they're not bound to tracks." Many predicted a low ridership for light-rail. It should be noted that, out of the twenty four largest metropolitan areas in the country, Minneapolis/St. Paul was the twenty third to have light rail transit, just before Cleveland, Ohio. When any metro area argued against light rail, they used the same four arguments you see above.

After a long battle, Ventura won and a light-rail system was built from the Minneapolis/St. Paul Airport to the famous Mall of America, then on to downtown Minneapolis. One year after it opened, ridership was 150% higher than predicted. Why? Emotion. It is cool to ride a train. It isn't cool to ride a bus. When people say, "I have to catch my train," it sounds better than, "I have to catch a bus."

On an unrelated note: the argument that a bus can drive anywhere, so it is a better option than transit stuck to a rail is common, but inaccurate. When busses were first introduced to metropolitan areas, they replaced trolleys. Everyone thought that, since a bus can drive anywhere, they were a more flexible option. After decades of use, it has been discovered that all bus routes mirror the rail routes formerly used by trolleys. It became clear that, even though busses can go anywhere, it doesn't make sense to drive them everywhere. Good mass transit relies on creating hubs that are convenient for the highest number of riders, which is what trolleys did in the first place.

Why all this talk about SUV's and light-rail trains? **Emotion versus fact is the single most important factor to successful networking.** If people like you, they will work with you. They will even invent reasons to work with you.

However, if you don't create a positive connection, no amount reason will get you in the door.

This seems like a simple concept, but most people network using a fact-based approach. This book will ask you to switch to focus more on feeling and intuition. Facts are important, just at the right time and place; and always *after* you have used emotion to market yourself.

The Two C's

Another principle that applies to networking is *The Two Cs of Marketing*. The two Cs are Comprehensive and Consistent. People have to see you *everywhere* and *all the time*. Dropping the ball on either of these two elements will diminish your success.

Take chambers of commerce, for example. The majority of people join a chamber because they think the networking opportunities are going to result in more business. They mistakenly think that organizations like chambers or professional associations come with a built-in loyalty factor that guarantees business. These people will attend a few meetings, shake a few hands, describe their service during the brief *introduce yourself* sessions, and then sit back and wait for the phone to ring. They assume that the office staff at the association is on the phone every day making sure that every member is sending business to every other member. If you speak to a staff member of a chamber of commerce you would discover that most of their time is spent recruiting new members to make up for the ones that quit when they discovered that simply becoming a member doesn't solve all of their problems.

Comprehensive means being everywhere; you can't just join one chamber and think your networking is covered. For some, this means joining more than one professional association. For others, associations won't result in any new business. You have to determine why an organization is a fit before you join. If associations aren't a good fit, think about where else can you be seen. This is where you need to be creative. You have to be seen *everywhere* in order to stand out from the crowd.

One form of networking I employ is being a columnist. I started writing a monthly column for the Business Journal Newspapers with one goal in mind; be seen. I started in 1997 and have since been nationally syndicated and the column appears in video format as well. Sometimes I get incoming calls for business because someone read something in my column that speaks directly to an issue their company is facing. Even if the column doesn't lead to direct business, when my name comes before a committee for consideration, someone usually says, "Oh yeah. I've heard of Stevie Ray." That is often all that is needed to be put on top of the list. And even though I began writing the column as a marketing tool, having to provide content that is of interest to business leaders across the country has kept me doing my homework. Now I read more and expose myself to more information than ever before. This has had immeasurable impact on my growth as a professional. What a great unexpected benefit. The thought of attaching a brand to yourself might seem a bit phony, but you are, in a sense, trying to accomplish the same goal as a company selling a product. Having a deadline every month means I am meeting the *consistent* requirement for marketing as well. Not everyone has the means or opportunity to pen a column, but with a little creative thinking you can find a way to keep yourself in front of people everywhere, all the time.

Just as important as being seen everywhere is being seen *all the time*. Being consistent means you can't get lazy. You can't attend two or three association meetings and expect the phone to ring. There is a reason people admire the woman who has volunteered to sit on the board of the association as well as run a committee or two. She is working hard and putting herself out there. The funny thing is, we are jealous when we discover how much business she gets and wonder why the universe doesn't smile on us like that. In networking, the universe helps those who help themselves.

Branding Yourself

No company sells a product without first determining its brand; how it will be positioned in the marketplace. When an automobile company markets a new car, they can't just say, "This is a Lexus. It is a really great car. Buy it." They have to give the Lexus an identity. This identity does not just involve what the car represents in terms of features and doodads; the identity also includes what the car is *not*. Essentially, the car is not like the bad things the competition offers. In the case of a Lexus, you are *not* getting what the competition offers, which is a boring, same-old driving experience. (No, the Toyota Company is not subsidizing this book. And I don't drive a Lexus.)

When networking, you are trying to accomplish the same goal as the car company; get the buyer excited about you while distinguishing yourself from the competition. People can't get excited about you until we know who you are and what you mean to us. That is the essence of branding.

Because branding seeks to distinguish the product from every other choice on the market, establishing your brand through networking is a challenge. There are dozens, if not hundreds, of others just like you; all competing for the same piece of mental real estate in the prospect's mind. It is vital that you stand apart from the crowd. *Distinguishing yourself from other networkers is likely the most difficult challenge you will face.*

The classic sales approach for decades has focused on *features, benefits,* and *advantages*. What features make the product stand out, what benefits the product provides the user, and the advantages of buying from this particular company. Sales professionals were told that, if they employed this very simple method, their sales would improve. This construct, like most simplified approaches to a problem, was widely accepted; not because it is particularly effective, but because it was easy to understand. If a sale was made using this method, the method was given the credit. If a sales professional lost a sale, they were blamed for not using the *features, benefits, advantages* approach effectively; they were usually retrained in the method.

As with many theories, it was nearly impossible to fully test the *features, benefits, advantages* theory because there is almost no way to provide a controlled study. And so, in true American fashion, what sounded reasonable, and what was repeated often enough, became fact. However, like so many other facts—we only use 10% of our brain, humans have five senses, and it is possible to win an argument with a teenager—the fact isn't true. Even though there is no real way to provide a controlled study of *features, benefits, advantages* over other sales/persuasion methods, we have something better; brain scans, and controlled studies of the human decision making process.

Modern medical technology allows us to scan the brain in ways never before possible. We can now actually see which parts of the brain activate during certain situations. This allows us to know whether the brain is accepting information or rejecting it (remember the Approach/Withdraw Response?). This, along with advanced studies in the psychology of decision making, illuminate a simple fact; the old axiom of marketing is true, *People buy with emotion, and justify with fact.* Emotions drive our every decision.

We buy certain clothes, cars, or household items because we feel good about them (or fear feeling bad about not having them). After buying something, however, we have to justify the purchase to someone else. The answer to, "Why did you choose A over B?" is rarely, "I don't know. I just felt good about it." We use facts to justify our decisions; "It gets great gas mileage," or "It fit the décor of the house perfectly." Feelings come first, intellect follows. This is why the *features, benefits, advantages* approach is weak. It does provide facts, which can help justify a decision, but it doesn't jazz up the emotional parts of the brain, which make the decision in the first place. Essentially, the *features, benefits, advantages* approach makes a critical error in judging the workings of the human brain, it assumes that we are primarily a logical being. It assumes we make decisions by weighing pros and cons and making an informed decision as a result of careful thought. Anyone who has an old pair of *Zubas* in their bottom drawer knows this assumption is flawed.

The reason we rarely weigh pros and cons is that doing so requires the highest levels of the brain to activate. The pre-frontal cortex is the part of the brain responsible for executive decision making. It was the last part of the brain to evolve, it is what makes us ultimately human, and it doesn't like to work. In fact, the least efficient function of the human brain is data processing. Processing information demands a high amount of energy, which is why reading a book puts us to sleep, while watching reality TV shows keep us awake. One requires thought, the other requires the absence of reason.

The most efficient function of the human brain is *pattern recognition*. The brain loves to discern patterns because pattern-seeking behavior has kept humans alive for millennia. Finding patterns and following patterned behavior has enabled humans to replicate behavior that kept us fed, safe, and productive. Pattern-seeking is a low-brain activity. It requires no real thought or attention. Emotional reaction is part of the patterned, reactive centers of the brain, and they dictate our decision making in powerful ways.

Because the *features, benefits, advantages* method requires participation of the pre-frontal cortex, it has the smallest chance of being accepted by the brain. By first creating an emotional connection, the pattern-seeking part of the brain kicks into gear. Once the brain is fully invested in what you have to say, then you can start talking details. But remember, since data processing tires out the brain, you have to keep this part of the conversation short.

Given all this, the goal of branding is not to get the buyer to *know* something about the product, but to get the buyer to *feel* something about the product. In order to do this, the manufacturer, and networker, has to go beyond simply inciting an emotional reaction on the part of the buyer, he or she has to know specifically which emotion to incite; which emotion is attached to their product. This is called the *Brand Emotion*. (As you continue reading, the information I provide on brand emotions is only one of many theories. Get five marketing experts in a room and you'll get six different opinions. I chose to present the most common theory, and the theory that best served the purpose of networking.)

If you look at any product on the market—clothing, food, beauty products—they all fall into one of five brand emotions: Sophistication, Trustworthy, Excitement, Competence, and Ruggedness. Even products within the same industry can fall into different emotional categories. Some blue jeans are branded as rugged, others are sophisticated, while others are exciting. But here is the catch, you can't have more than one emotion attached to a product. If two emotions are attached to any product, the resulting confusion cancels them altogether. Campbell's soup is trustworthy, it cannot also be competent. There are other soups that use the competent brand emotion by touting the healthy vitamins and minerals and USDA approved blah blah blah, but they cannot include the sincerity of "Mmmm mmmm good." When promoting your service, you have to choose which emotion you represent, and stick to it.

The difficulty in trying determine which of the five emotions we represent is the fear that we will drive away business from people seeking a different emotion. You want that new job, that promotion, or that new opportunity. The more desperate we are, the more we try to be all things to all people. If someone needs a *competent* person, we say, "That's me! I'm competent." If they want someone with exciting ideas, "That's me, too." And if they want someone who is tough, "I'm your man!" As much as it might feel phony to brand yourself, it is even more disingenuous to try to be all things to all people. And, as the old saying goes, *If you try to be everything to everyone, you'll end up being nothing to no one.*

Years ago we were struggling with the brand emotion of Stevie Ray's Improv Company. We were marketing our corporate workshops as Competent, the comedy shows were Excitement, and the skills-training classes for the public were Trustworthy. Even though we were capable of being each emotion (as is any person or business), we were so busy chasing the emotion that attracted a particular client on a particular day, that we weren't being true to ourselves. We hadn't decided who we truly were. Each emotion was fighting the other. After speaking with clients and colleagues we discovered that the overarching brand emotion of our company, no matter what the specific service being provided, was excitement. Now we use that emotion in describing all of our services. Having a single emotion, a singular image, makes it easier for clients, audience members, and students to understand who we are and what we represent.

Sure, human beings are far too complicated to be confined to such a limited identity. People can be rugged, exciting, and sophisticated all at once. I like the quote by author Robert Heinlein, *Specialization is for insects*. However, when we first meet you we have to know the clear, simple version of what we are buying. Determining which emotion best represents you not only helps the other person know who you are, but, more importantly, how you can help them. And good networking all comes down to showing people how you can be of service to them.

If you are at a loss as to how to determine your brand emotion, just ask others what they think of you. Don't leave this step to yourself. To be honest, wouldn't most of us assign ourselves a "cool" emotion, even if another one might be more accurate? Ask your friends which of those five emotions best describes you. Ask colleagues and past clients to think about competence, trustworthy, exciting, sophisticated, or rugged; and decide which reminds them of you the most. Assure them you won't take their answer personally or be offended by their choice. Also remind them that they are not summing your entire personality into one word, just the service you provide. Once you have the emotion in hand, represent yourself consistently with that brand.

The Art of Persuasion

It is no secret that the art of networking is, in a nutshell, the art of persuasion. And, as we discussed in the section about branding, the art of persuasion is more complicated than simply listing the attributes of your product or service. Fortunately, we are able to break down the process of persuasion into easy-to-understand steps. Easy to understand, yes; but to be able to employ them takes practice. First, let's distinguish between the two major approaches to persuasion.

The two main approaches to persuasion are distinguished by how they manage the two elements to any persuasive argument; the facts, and the conclusion. One approach to persuasion states the conclusion first, followed by facts to support the conclusion; the other approach reverses the order. The first approach—"Here is what I want you to do, now here is why you should do it."—is the most commonly used. Pay attention to any argument, debate, or decision-making meeting and you will hear this in practice. As easy as this approach is to use, it is only effective a small percentage of the time. The reason is, *conclusion followed by facts only works when the audience/listener is already in agreement with you.*

The single goal of any persuasive argument, and for networking, is to get the other person to say "yes" as often as possible. Psychologists have discovered that the more frequently a person says "yes" during a conversation, the more difficult it is to switch gears at the very end and say "no" to the final request. Getting a "yes" requires knowing whether the other person is going to be resistant to your message from the outset.

If you attend a high school pep rally or political convention, you will see the conclusion-first approach in full force. Because the audience at both these events is already in agreement with the conclusion, the conclusion comes first. "We're the best school ever, right?" "Yes!" Now that the conclusion is firmly in place, the facts follow; "Because we have the best students, right?" "Yes!" "And the best teachers, right?" "Yes!" "And the…" This goes on until the crowd is called to action; whether to cheer on a sports team or vote for a political candidate.

The problem is, if you use the conclusion-first approach with an audience that is either neutral or against your message, you lose. Stating the conclusion to a person who is against your message sets in place a brick wall that no argument can break down. Imagine if you neighbor knocked on your door and said, "I would like you to babysit my kids for a month while I am out of town. Now here is why I think this is a good idea…" The entire time your neighbor is listing the reasons for babysitting his kids, you are thinking, "This will happen when pigs fly." Stating the conclusion to a resistant audience ensures that, not only does listening stop, but they expend all their mental energy on creating comebacks for the reasons you state.

If you are unsure as to the position of your listener, or you know they are against your message, you must use the second approach; facts leading up to a conclusion. Because most people distrust car sales professionals, this is the approach used in car sales transactions. When selling you a car, the salesperson's goal is to get as many yes responses from you as possible. And here is the kicker, the yes doesn't even have to relate to the car you are considering. Psychologists have discovered that a yes of any kind, about anything, leads us down the path of cooperation.

This is why the car dealer will ask, "Nice day today, isn't it?" If you say yes, you are one step closer to buying the car. The entire conversation—during the initial look-see, the test drive, and the negotiation—is designed to keep you saying yes. Want another kicker? A physical yes is as powerful as a verbal one. If the dealer asks you to sit down to talk over the car, often he or she will wait for you to start sitting and then say, "Here, why don't you sit over here and I'll take that chair." If you agree to switch chairs, the physical yes triggers a cooperative attitude, and you are more likely to buy the car. There is no difference between one chair and another, the dealer just needs a physical yes from you.

How does this affect your networking approach? You can't start by saying, "I have the best printing company in town, and here is why." Unless we are already familiar with your printing company, and agree that it is the best in town, you have set yourself up for distrust and disagreement. You must first get some yes responses, then lead to the conclusion that you are the best option.

This approach can certainly appear manipulative, and if you have ever walked off a car dealership lot holding keys to a car you didn't intend to buy, it can be used in ways that don't serve all parties involved. But here is why facts-first is actually less manipulative than the conclusion-first approach. If you begin a conversation with an end result firmly in mind, you leave no room for compromise. If the only option in my mind is that you need to babysit my children, any other option is dismissed. Conclusion-first sets you on the path of no compromise. If, however, you start with facts that both parties can agree on, and work toward a natural conclusion, the end result might be different than what you expected, but still be good for both parties. With the facts-first approach, you are in a greater position to listen, consider, and incorporate others' ideas.

Human nature requires that the art of persuasion be approached by offering to solve someone else's problem, not asking them to solve yours. This runs counter to how most people network. The "Let me give you my business card. I would like to talk to you about my business" approach is all about you, and is poor networking. It also ignores another important psychological fact about humans; *people move more quickly away from pain than they do toward pleasure.*

The conclusion-first approach almost always involves the positive outcome you promise to provide. Humans, however, do not often trust promises of positive outcomes. This is because we are less concerned with finding pleasure than we are avoiding pain. If you remember from earlier in the book, the brain's default mechanism is keeping its host safe from harm. This means the brain is more concerned with avoiding danger than finding pleasure. So it is more effective to say, "I will help you avoid problems" than "I will make your life great."

Robert Middleton, an expert in marketing professional services and author of *Infoguru Marketing*, reminds us that marketing a professional service is different than marketing a retail product. When marketing a retail product, you talk mainly about the product (somewhat like the *features, benefits, advantages* approach), but with a professional service, you talk about the pain you will help the other person avoid. Without a pain statement, the other person sees no urgent need in working with you.

When people used to ask Middleton about his work, he would respond, "I help market professional service providers so they can get more clients." He discovered that this approach resulted in two reactions on the part of the listener: 1) "Oh, you're just like that other guy" and 2) "I'm fine. I don't need that." When you simply describe your service in terms of outcome, people immediately lump you in with everyone else who provides the same service, "Oh, you are one of *those* people." It isn't necessarily a bad reaction, but you immediately lose any specialness about you. You become a commodity, and therefore judged on price.

The other reaction, "I don't need you," is based on the fact that, when you talk about outcomes, people don't see a need for themselves. However, when you talk about problems, people think they have them even if they don't. This is probably why medical students seem to be afflicted with whatever disease they are studying that week. Now, when Middleton is asked about his business, he replies, "I help market professional services providers who *struggle* to get all the clients *they need*." He uses phrases like "struggle," "have difficulty with," or "stressed about." Humans are funny. As soon as we hear about a problem, we think the problem is ours.

Look at most TV commercials. If you ask most people if they own enough credit cards, they would say they are fine. When a commercial says, "Get the credit you deserve," we suddenly think good enough is no longer good enough. "Do you struggle with hair loss?" sells more Rogaine than, "Get a nice head of thick hair." And home security systems sell more when the message is "Don't be the victim!" And political parties have long used the time-tested tactic of negative spin. If a political party is not in power, all statements during the election point to how terrible life is for every American. The party that is in power has to convince us that life is actually pretty good. And convincing people that their life is bad is a lot easier.

Examine how you talk about your product or service and make sure you are solving a problem, not promising pleasure. The next step is to present your case in a fashion that the brain can most easily absorb. This is where the Five

Steps of Persuasion comes in. If you present a persuasive argument in the right order, and include all five steps, your chances for networking success greatly improve. The five steps are: The Hook, The Problem, The Solution, The Details and The Action.

The Hook

The first step involves finding what is of most interest to the other person so they feel compelled to listen. Television commercials get us to buy stuff we wouldn't normally buy by immediately hooking us, "Would you like to earn more money?" This question may seem corny, and we may see it as an obvious hook, but we still put down the remote and listen. After all, the TV sponsor has to keep you from jumping up to make a sandwich during the commercial.

In networking, the hook is less blatant, but no less important. Sometimes the hook is simply expressing an interest in the other person's business or life. People so rarely get the chance to be heard that expressing a genuine interest in them is a real hook.

Another hook is laughter. Laughter is a powerful tool of social bonding. In fact, the majority of laughter is not at the result of something funny, but instead a way for a group to connect. For his book, *Laughter: A Scientific Investigation*, Dr. Robert Provine had researchers track laughter in everyday life. They observed people at coffee shops, parties, offices, and get-togethers. Using a sophisticated metrics, they tracked when laughter occurred, what was said to inspire the laughter, who did the speaking, who did the laughing, and how long the laughter lasted. Sure sounds like a process that would take the fun out of the research, right?

What Provine discovered was the majority of laughter was to express agreement. Common phrases that accompanied laughter were, "You got that right!" or "The same thing happened to me." Laughter is such a powerful tool, and signal, of agreement that it is nearly impossible to laugh and disagree with someone at the same time.

Many people are nervous when it comes to being funny. They see a professional comedian and think, "I'm not as funny as that guy," so they give up. The beauty of humor is that, even if you don't get a big laugh, people appreciate the attempt at humor so much that you still gain social standing. The only caveat is, if you try for humor and it doesn't work, you cannot show defeat or nervousness. The mere attempt at humor is enough to build your social capital, but showing nervousness destroys that capital in a hurry.

The other truth is, few people are as funny *on stage* as a professional comedian, but that isn't your goal anyway. Humor in networking doesn't involve keeping a roomful of people in stitches. It involves light-hearted, friendly conversation that produces a connectedness that is expressed through laughter. So put away the joke book, put yourself out there, and laugh along with the group.

And remember, the point of good networking is to create an atmosphere in which your partner doesn't want to leave the conversation. No-one ever laughs during a conversation and thinks, "I hate having all this fun. When can I get out of here?" Don't make conversation stiff or nervous, hook your partner by lightening the mood. However, although laughter is a fantastic tool of the Hook stage, you can't simply pull laughter out of your pocket. You have to employ techniques that inspire laughter *while* hooking your partner. And the best technique is to *tell a story*.

Research in persuasive theory tested three main methods of persuasion; 1) deliver pertinent facts, 2) tell a story, 3) tell a story that is backed up by facts. Of the three methods, the most effective was to tell a story, all by itself. This was a surprise to those who thought that combining the two methods would deliver a one-two punch; sealing the argument for sure. If you remember from earlier in the book that people buy with emotion and justify with fact, then facts certainly have their place.

It is not that facts have no place in persuasion, or networking, it is just that they must be placed where they can do the most good. Stories carry more persuasive oomph than stories combined with facts because attempting to bolster the point of a story actually detracts from the story's authenticity. It is sort of like listening to someone tell you a funny happening in their life, but they keep saying, "This is a true story. This really happened." You were willing to believe in the story until they tried to prove it was real.

Stories are a great hooking device for two reasons; one we already discussed, people tend to believe stories are true. The other hook-y quality of a story is *people have to hear the end of the story*. There is a quirky quality among humans that, once a story has begun, we have to stay until the end to learn the outcome. Have you ever watched a terrible TV show, but you watched it until the end just because you had to see how things turned out? (For me, it was *The Bachelor*. Guess who had control of the remote that night.)

Inserting a story into networking is easy, and it actually acts as a blocker for you saying the wrong thing. For instance, if your partner says, "I have been having the worst time trying to figure out my year-end what's-it." Your urge would be to say, "I just so happened to be an expert in what's-it. Let's schedule a meeting." To be fair, this approach may sometimes work, but you rely on the chance that your partner is receptive. If, however, you say, "I know a guy who had that same problem. Do you want to know what he did?" your partner is riveted. They not only want to know how the plot was resolved, but they know that the answer to their problems is within the story. Of course, the smart networking storyteller will make sure he or she is included in the story so the partner can connect the dots and see you as someone to get to know.

Stories employ another powerful tool, a psychological process called *social proof*. Social proof is the feeling that if something worked for someone else, it will work for you. The fact that humans are a social animal means that we believe what other people experience will result in the same experience for us. This is why testimonials work so well for selling products on TV commercials. Notice the next time someone who is *not an actor* touts the great qualities of laundry detergent. Mostly likely, the *non-actor* will look like he or she could be your neighbor. In order for social proof to work, the person giving the testimonial must be similar in demographic qualities as the prospect.

The power of social proof, and social decision making, was tested in an enlightening experiment. Neighborhoods throughout California were surveyed and the residents were asked which approach they thought would be most effective in getting them to lower their usage of household electricity.
1) Using less electricity is better for the environment and would leave a better world for the next generation. (Moral incentive)
2) Using less electricity saves money. (Financial incentive)
3) All their neighbors are employing the electricity-saving techniques. (Social incentive)

No one likes to admit that they do things just because others do it first, so the majority of responses fell in the order of:
1) Moral
2) Financial
3) Social

People wanted to be seen as concerned for the environment before being money-hungry. And no one wanted to be viewed as just following the crowd. For the second stage of the test, researchers went to new neighborhoods and left fliers at people's homes that explained steps to reduce electricity usage. Some neighborhoods received fliers that explained the environmental impact of saving electricity, others explained the financial benefit to the homeowner, while other fliers simply said, "All your neighbors are doing this." By approaching entire neighborhoods with one of the three incentives, the researchers were able to track actual electric usage to determine which incentive worked best; moral, financial, or social.

When the results were tallied, social incentives far outpaced the other two; with financial incentives outdoing moral incentives. Sorry, we just aren't as upstanding as we like to think we are. What this means for networking is your story should include statements like, "I worked with another company just like yours, and here is what we did for them." Rather than pushing how great you are, let examples of your previous work speak for you. I experience the power of social proof quite often when I speak with prospective clients. A concern of many clients is "Have you worked with other companies just like ours?" I am often asked by law firms to list other law firms that have hired me. The same holds true for hospitals, schools, banks, you name it. I am booked more frequently when I can provide examples of previous clients in the industry.

Practicing stories is simple. During casual conversations, relate experiences by delivering an engaging introduction, a body of the story that includes only as much detail as is necessary for the listeners to understand the plot, then button it up with an ending that either contains a lesson or a laugh. Give others a plot, or storyline, to follow that will keep them engaged. And make sure there is a lesson at the end. You don't need to pound the lesson home, you just have to have one.

The Problem

This step calls for you to illuminate a problem in the other person's life. This is where a lot of people make mistakes in networking because instead of focusing on their partner, they talk about their own problems or needs. "I'm looking for people who need financial advice." If you focus only on your problems we may feign interest, but we're just being polite. What we really want to talk about is our own life and our own issues. Get your networking prospect to talk about his or her business, career, or life and eventually they will share a challenge they are facing. Your task is to listen intently, so they open up and share what is keeping them up at night with worry. Then, as the conversation progresses, you must increase the urgency of the problem. You must get the prospect to ponder "What will keep getting worse if something isn't done about this problem?" Talking about problems gets your partner connected to you. Adding urgency ensures that they will want to stay connected with you in order to find a solution before it is too late.

Urgency comes in many forms, and you will see them used to great effect in advertising. Urgency goes hand-in-hand with scarcity. The classic uses of urgency/scarcity are *time*, "Time is running out. Act now!" *resources*, "There are only a few of these left in our warehouse, so you'd better act now!" and *information*, "Learn the secrets that celebrity hair stylists have kept to themselves for years." Take a moment to examine what qualities you have about your business that create an urgent need on the part of your customer.

Once you have your prospect eager to solve a problem and with a sense of urgency, now you can move on to the third step.

The Solution

This is where you shine. Now is when you talk about how your business can help the prospect. If you have ideas to offer about their problem or can steer him in the right direction for a solution, you become his best friend. Naturally you want the solution to be *you*, but that might not always be the case, nor is it necessary in order to make networking beneficial for you. If you offer solutions to other people's problems, they will remember you as a valuable resource, not just a service to be used and then forgotten.

The Details

This is the who, what, where, and how of the solution. Don't spend any more time here than you have to. Frankly, this step bores most people. It is common for detail-oriented professions—engineers, accountants, technicians—to get too deep in the details when talking about what they do. The truth is, even if people ask for details, they don't really want to know. When people ask, "Oh really, how do you do that?" it is often the only thing they know to say at the moment. Details are hard to digest and difficult to remember. Too much data shuts down the brain. If we ask for details, what we really want is the big picture.

The brain loves to categorize. So any details you provide should avoid a long string of facts, and instead come in easy-to-digest clumps. If you remember from earlier in the book, the brains most efficient function is pattern recognition; and it is especially fond of patterns of three. If you were asked to remember ten numbers, 9525009230, your brain would freeze up. However, clump those same digits into a grouping of three, 952-500-9230, and you have an area code, prefix, and telephone number; the clumping into threes makes remembering it easier.

The thing about memory, if something becomes too difficult to remember, we simply choose to clear it from our brain. So don't tell the prospect anything more than three quick take-aways, it will make you easier to remember. If there is any more information, offer to send the information later. This ensures future contact, which is what you want anyway.

The Action

This step, also called the *Call to Action*, is the one of the most ignored elements of persuasion. We usually just hope we have engaged the other person's interest enough that they will call. In fact, most people only use two of the five steps. They start with the solution, then give a bunch of details, than sit back and wait. Once, a guy handed me his business card and said, "Call if you need computer assistance." Naturally I said, "Sure," and threw his card away later.

For an action step to work it must be specific. You must give a time and date by when the action must take place.

"The next time you are shopping for software, think of me" is not an action step. There is no specific time or date, which leaves your next encounter ambiguous, and up in the air. An action step should be definite, "I know someone who can help you with that problem. I'll call you Friday at 3:00 p.m. and we can set up a meeting." Now your partner knows exactly what to expect.

Some people are hesitant to give an action step because they are afraid of appearing pushy or demanding. Of course, you don't want to be too forceful with your action step, but providing clarity in the form of a time, date, and action doesn't create stress, it relieves it. Not knowing what will happen next, or what to do, leaves people unsure of their role in the relationship. Your willingness to provide forward momentum and guidance toward that end positions you as a leader; someone we can trust to get things done.

Don't rule out giving the other person a specific action. "When you get back to your office, take a look at your interest rates and call me by the end of the day. I'll let you know if I can get you a better deal." Asking someone to *think* about something is not an action, and produces no results. An action must be a physical act your partner can take, and must include a means for you to reconnect. The best way to think about the action step is to ask yourself "Can the action be counted and tracked?" A phone call is a countable action, by 3:00 p.m. is a means of tracking. You can't count how many times someone thinks about something, and you certainly can't track it.

As I mentioned earlier, the best way to hone your skills is to practice them in non-networking situations. See if you can employ the five steps when deciding where to have lunch with friends, or which TV show to watch with your spouse or partner. It takes time to make the five-step process a natural part of your conversation, so don't wait until the next networking event to practice.

Now that we have covered the Five Steps of Persuasion, let's add some techniques to make them more effective.

Be Memorable

One of the most important, and challenging, goals of networking is to stand apart from others. To be memorable. There are hundreds of people clamoring for the same attention you seek. They all want to own the same small piece of mental real estate in the mind of the prospect. After you have met someone and chatted for a while, how can you be sure they will remember you? How can you be sure that what they remember is what you *want* them to remember?

I was working with a young lady on her networking skills and I asked her, "What do people remember most about you?" She said, "Well, I *hope* they remember that I am..." And in that word, hope, was the problem. She didn't control what people remembered, she left it to chance. What people remember about you cannot be left to chance. The good news is, you have more influence over other people's memory than you might think.

Memory is influenced by three factors, Primacy, Frequency, and Urgency. **Primacy**: we remember the first and last thing we experience. Typically, the last thing we experience in a situation is easier to remember than the first because it is a more recent occurrence. **Frequency**: the more we experience something, the more it becomes a pattern in our brain. Memories are simple neural patterns.

We have little control over the first two factors. We can't really control whether we are the first or last person our prospect meets at a networking function or during the day. We could try to influence this element, but there are laws against stalking. We can try to employ repetition by repeating our name over and over again, but if you recall how TV commercials repeat the toll-free phone number a dozen times during the commercial, you recognize the fine line between repetition and redundancy. One aids in memory, the other is annoying.

We do have control over the third element, **Urgency**: the more important something is to us, the more we will remember it. And, as is true with scarcity, urgency doesn't have to be real in order to be effective. *Perceived urgency* is just as effective as the actual thing. If it wasn't, most of the junk peddled on TV would still be sitting on a shelf in a warehouse.

Influencing Behavior

A great example of perceived urgency is illustrated in the book, *Influence: Science and Practice* by Robert Cialdini. Cialdini is a Regents' Professor of Psychology at Arizona State University who made a multi-year study on the factors that most influence human behavior. The factor of urgency was one of the most important influences.

In one of Cialdini's tests, university students were asked to rate cookies on taste, texture, and overall yumminess. One group of students were given a large jar of cookies. They were asked to sample a cookie and complete a questionnaire. The students gave the cookies a variety of satisfaction scores, from average to very good. The next set of tasters, however, were only given one cookie to sample instead of an entire jar. Even though the cookies were the same in both tests, the students who were only given one cookie gave higher satisfaction ratings.

In a final test, a third set of students were given a large jar of cookies, but as soon as they took one cookie from the jar a researcher entered the room and said, "If you already have a cookie to taste we're going to take the jar to another group down the hall. They really like them and want more." The group that had cookies, but had them taken away reported such high satisfaction scores that they asked if they could have the rest of the cookies when the other group was done. In all three tests, the cookies remained the same, only the urgency changed. It is worth noting that the third test was likely influenced by *social proof*, since the tasters were told that another group really liked the cookies.

Cialdini proved that we decide how much we value something based on urgency, and that perceived urgency is just as powerful as the real thing. This affects networking in profound ways. If, while networking, you appear overly eager to make a connection with someone, there is obviously no need for the prospect to act immediately, if at all. You are not *in limited supply* so there is no urgency to work with you. You will obviously be available whenever the prospect feels like reaching out, so your name goes to the bottom of the list. If, however, you are *hard to get,* they will not only be more eager to work with you, but they are likely to give you higher satisfaction scores. This is why it is not a good idea to tell someone to "call me at your convenience." It makes it seem like you are waiting by the phone. I will often tell prospects that I am unavailable Monday through Wednesday, but they can call me Thursday afternoon. You would be surprised how often Thursday afternoon rolls around and my phone rings.

    I tested this principle when a prospective client called to inquire about me conducting a workshop for their company. The woman said, "I'm calling to see if you are available on the 22nd to do a workshop for my employee group. How much do you charge?" Since she was calling to hire me, she naturally expected me to bend over backwards to please her. I surprised her by saying, "Well, before I accept the job I need to determine if it is a good fit for me. I am successful in my workshops because I make sure that I only work with groups that are a perfect fit for me." After a brief pause she said, "What kind of groups do you require." I said, "I only work with employees that are motivated to learn new techniques because they know it will improve their jobs. They have to have skin in the game. These are usually highly educated employees at the executive level. And I prefer not to work with people who are forced to attend my workshop.

Mandatory attendance works for some presentations, but not so well when you are teaching professional skill-building."

I could tell by her reaction that she was surprised at my list of requirements. She was probably accustomed to hearing trainers and speakers talk about how great their sessions were; but that can appear like the trainer is pleading for the work. I, on the other hand, was almost refusing to do the workshop if it wasn't to my liking. She responded, "If we promise to have those kinds of people at the session, would you be willing to do the workshop?" I said I would be more than happy if the conditions were right for a successful session.

We continued to discuss her goals and how I could meet them. The conversation ended with her asking me to send a contract. She hung up the phone without even asking my fee. I had created such urgency in her mind that, no matter what my fee was, she was going to find the money. There was more to the conversation, but I will delve deeper later in the book. For now, we'll just discuss the fact that my new client didn't ask about the fee. Any good salesperson will tell you that the decision not to buy is rarely based on cost. Money isn't the reason people don't buy, it is just the easiest excuse. If you create enough need, real or perceived, the money will be found.

While networking, describe what qualities *you* require before you will accept a job. If someone asks if you are free for a meeting, tell them you have a pretty full schedule, but can fit them in on specific days and times. Never give the impression you are looking for any possible opportunity; but that you are only interested in the right opportunity. Be the *limited supply, call now, only a few left in our warehouse* person.

The Psychology of the Listener

It may seem like networking conversations have a life of their own; that you are subject to the whims and emotions of the others you meet. However, while networking, you are actually responsible for the state of mind of the person you are talking to. You may think others are distracted because they have a lot on their mind, but that is not always the case. If someone is distracted, it is because you aren't more important than the other things they have on their mind. If others seem bored, it is because you are boring. If they seem intrigued, it is because you are intriguing.

Humans are mammals, and all mammals are social creatures; meaning that the behavior of mammals is driven more by social influences than by individual desires. In fact, humans are so interconnected in our behavior that psychologists have labeled humans as *Ultra-Social Mammals*. We are more affected by group mentality than any other mammal on the planet.

Being mammals also leaves us with a certain wiring in the brain. All mammals live in one of two *states of being*. Which state we are in will drive our decision making. Mammals live in either a state of comfort or a state of nervousness. A state of comfort leads to attraction, trust, and a desire to connect further (either socially or professionally). A state of nervousness leads to distrust, dislike, and distance.

You can easily see the comfort/nervous behavior in a common mammal, the dog. When dogs are comfortable, they obey commands and allow other animals within their territory. When comfortable, a dog's ears lay back and the tail sways back and forth lazily or hangs down. If a dog experiences good nervousness, it creates excitement. "We're going for a walk!" The ears pick up and the tail wags quickly back and forth. However, bad nervousness, as happens when a stranger invades the territory, has the ears up as well as forward. The dog's hair on the back of the neck stands on end, and the tail shoots straight back with tension.

Because mammals are social creatures, the state of comfort or nervousness largely depends on the state of others in the group. And the leader of the group has immense impact of the state of being of every member in the group. Pack animals are keenly aware of the emotional state of the leader. Dog packs have an alpha dog. This dog, male or female, always walks in front of the pack as a look-out for danger. This is why the alpha shows signs of nervousness; he or she is looking out for danger. The dogs in the pack show signs of comfort because they are just following behind. If you watch a pack dog, their gait is even and their eyes look steadily forward, whereas the alpha's eyes dart back and forth; looking for any predators. Dog experts tell us that letting your dog walk in front of you signals to the dog that it is the alpha. This is why your dog is in a state of excitement. It is not the happy "we're out for a walk" excitement, it is the "my pack is behind me so I better look for danger" nervousness. This is also why many dogs don't obey their masters while on a walk. The alpha is the lead dog, and the lead dog doesn't take orders.

My wife, Kanitta, loves to let our Jack Russell Terrier, Pepper, walk in front. As he stretches to the limit of his leash, he is all over the place. His tail is tense and no other creature passes by without a thorough inspection. Kanitta always says, "Look at how happy Pepper is!" I respond, "He is not happy. He is freaking out! He is sure there is a wolf in our neighborhood, and he is protecting us from it." When it is my turn to hold the leash, I follow the experts' advice, I hold the leash so Pepper walks just behind me. The transformation is instant. As soon as Pepper sees my legs walk in front of him, his gait evens out and his eyes look straight ahead. Complete state of comfort. I can almost hear him say to himself, "Whew! Let this dude handle the wolf."

In order to be perceived as a trusted new connection, people need to feel that they can put themselves safely in your hands. You must be the alpha that protects them. And remember, alphas protect, they do not dominate. A dominating personality is just as off-putting as a weak one.

Because humans are more mentally complex than other mammals, we have a third state of being that other mammals do not; the state of extreme comfort. Extreme comfort is just as bad as nervousness because extreme comfort leads to complacency. Complacency is dangerous because it results in a complete lack of urgency on the part of your prospect. Essentially, networking requires that you create just the right balance of the three states of being. Too much comfort: they don't need you. Not enough comfort: they don't like you.

Too much nervousness, they don't trust you. The best balance is a mixture of excitement—"What new thing are you bringing into my life?" —and comfort—"I trust that you won't lead me astray, abandon me, or lie to me."

Not an easy balance to strike, to be sure. That is why you cannot fake good networking. If you aren't willing to show your genuine self, the rest of the pack will sense it. We are all like dogs, we can smell dishonesty, and we don't respond well to it. But if you bring your genuine personality, with a commanding presence, we will let you into the pack.

CHAPTER 2

The Real Opportunities

No book on networking would be complete without a discussion about *where* you should network. The majority of business opportunities are indeed gained through face-to-face networking, but it is no secret that networking does not have to occur at formal functions.

Remember the two C's of marketing? *Comprehensive* and *Consistent* means that people need to see you everywhere, all the time. Since it is unlikely that you are going to rent a billboard with your face on it so that people can see you every day on their way to work, comprehensive and consistent refers to the manner in which you approach networking itself; *everywhere* and *all the time*. Side note: a young man seeking employment in Minneapolis actually did rent a billboard with his face on it with the caption that he was looking for work. He was offered a job within a few days.

This is the point when many people think, "There is no way I'm going to become one of those pushy people who shake everyone's hand in the grocery store line and talk about their business." I certainly hope not, at least not while

I'm standing in line with you. Good networking is not about asking people to give to you, it is about you being of value to those around you. Being comprehensive and consistent doesn't mean that you see every person as a prospect, it means that you keep your social skills sharp with consistent networking that is comprehensive in its scope. So the benefit of comprehensive networking is not solely to gain new business, it is also to use those interactions to improve your own skills.

Social skills are more difficult to hone than technical skills, so keeping them sharp requires paying attention to the social environment you find yourself in, and practicing these skills whenever possible. Even the briefest, and seemingly meaningless, social encounter is a chance to sharpen your ability to capture someone's attention, and engage them. Step One: *Whenever possible, opt for human interaction instead of electronic.* It is easy to carry on a conversation with friends and family because the brain loves familiarity. When encountering familiar, trusted people, the brain doesn't have to go through the tedious *Approach/Withdraw Response* evaluation.

Networking, typically involving strangers, is tougher. Simple social interaction requires a lot of brain power. In fact, many brain scientists claim that we can skip buying those *brain games* sold through TV commercials to improve our mental acuity. You can achieve the same result by engaging in more social interaction. That is how much impact speaking to strangers has on that three- pound mass of nervous tissue in our skull. Engaging with strangers may seem like an insignificant act to take when improving networking skills, but it is precisely because you are dealing with strangers, and using verbal interplay in the process, that this step is so beneficial.

Step B: *Turn transactional relationships into connected ones.* Transactional relationships are the everyday in-and-outs; the grocery store check-out, the bank clerk, or the floor assistant at a retail shop. They all consist of the same three steps; 1) How can I help you? 2) Here is what you wanted. 3) Bye-bye. There is no real human connection. You conduct business and move on. Sadly, this also describes most networking interactions. This is because too many people consider networking to be a game of acquiring *contacts* instead of making *contact*. Transactional relationships are a perfect practice-ground for two reasons; 1) no one is expecting anything more from the relationship, 2) it is not a consequential relationship.

Of course, no one going to the bank is expecting to make a new best friend, so neither the teller nor the customer places any great weight on the encounter. This makes the situation fertile ground for practicing communication skills. If you can shake someone out of their mental working zone and engage in conversation, however brief the encounter, you will sharpen your ability to speak to anyone. This practice shapes your brain to react without fear, hesitation, or panic when faced with strangers.

The second point is equally important, that fact that transactional relationships are not deeply consequential. This is not to say that the other person doesn't matter. Quite the contrary. I believe in the old advice given to people seeking a mate, *watch how they treat servers in a restaurant, because that is how they will ultimately treat you.* The reason you want to practice your skills during transactional encounters is because you don't want to wait until situations when real business can be won or lost.

No athlete says, "Darn! I lost the race. I guess I'll wait until the next race and try to do better." We would scoff at such an athlete, but this is precisely how most people approach networking. They stumble through a cocktail hour or business function, lament about the lack of success they had, and go back to business as usual until the next invitation is sent their way. How much more success would they achieve if they practiced a little bit every day? Without appearing boastful, I am personally known for being very good at meeting and engaging with new people. This wasn't always the case. Contrary to my step-daughter's opinion, I was once an actual teenager, with all the angst and self-doubt that this lovely period of human development provides. And many professional entertainers, of which I am one, will tell you that those who make their living being on the big stage can often be the quietest person at the after-show party.

How did I develop my legendary networking skills? By turning everyday encounters into practice sessions. I try to never waste a trip to the bank or the grocery store, or a phone call with a customer service rep. If I see a bank teller with a nice-looking neck-tie, I will offer a compliment. If a clerk asks (probably for the ninety-seventh time that day), "How is your day, today?" I never just say, "Fine." I will respond with something that will not allow a bland response.

Typical exchange:
Clerk: "And how is your day going?"
Customer: "Fine."
Clerk: "That's nice. Did you want the balance on this account?"

Connected exchange:
Clerk: "And how is your day going?"
Legendary Stevie Ray: "Pretty good. Other than I had to shovel the driveway at six a.m. so my wife could get to work. Do you have to shovel or are you an apartment dweller who gets to laugh at the rest of us?"
Clerk: (responds with conversation while thinking, "Boy, is this guy legendary!")

The difference between the two exchanges might not seem like much, but they are worlds apart in terms of developing communication skills, as well as wiring the brain to handle interactions with strangers with ease. The trap to avoid—and this is a big trap—is not to rely on the same banter over and over. Because the brain loves familiarity and patterns, it falls into habit very easily. So, a comment that works at the bank will be reused at the grocery store; and then at Target, and then…you get the picture. Reusing tried-and-true material works for a while. In fact, it isn't a bad idea to know what type of approach feels most comfortable for you, but repeating is not the same as creating. If you fall into the habit of using the same lines over and over again, you are not only cheating yourself out of valuable practice, you will hurt your chances of engaging people in meaningful conversations when real networking opportunities pop up. We have all met the person whose conversation just doesn't feel real. It is guaranteed that they have spoken these lines many times before.

The way to avoid this trap is to follow an old adage from the world of improvisation; *stay in the moment*. More about improvisation, or "improv," later, but staying in the moment refers to keeping one's focus on what is happening right now, instead of worrying about the outcome. The opposite of being *in the moment* is being *in your head*. Essentially, the more you worry about how an interaction might turn out, the more likely you are to sabotage the whole thing without even realizing it. When I was a young man and first learning the art of improvisation, I was practicing an exercise with a partner during class. At one point, the instructor stopped us and looked at me and said, "You are totally in your head, aren't you?" I admitted that I was. She asked, "Why. What are you thinking?" I said, "I was stressing out because I didn't know where this was going and how it was going to end."

The instructor said, "The more you worry about where you are going, the more you will ruin where you are." She looked at my exercise partner and said, "Could you tell that Stevie was in his head?" The partner said that, indeed, he could easily tell that my head wasn't in the game. She turned to me and said, "Not only did you take your head out of the game, by not focusing on the *right now*, your lack of focus forced your partner to lose focus." She ended with, "Remember when you were kids playing make-believe? One of you was the knight in armor and the other was the evil dragon. You could play for hours because neither of you worried about how it was going to end. Just play with your friend and everything will turn out fine."

Does this sound like some networking interactions you have had? Have you known in an instant when the other person was in their head instead of in the moment? That is the moment when trust is lost. Practicing making a connection by focusing on what is right in front of you, and doing it on a consistent basis during transactional relationships, is a great way to train for in-the-moment focus.

One more technique to employ during transactional relationships is humor. As we discussed earlier, humor and laughter are great hooks because of how they affect our thinking, but the ability to spark a laugh is not gained through genetics, it is a skill that can be practiced and perfected. And transactional relationships are a great place to practice humor because, remember, the relationship doesn't count. If you try for *the funny* with friends or colleagues, and it doesn't work, you not only feel like a fool, but you have to see these people again. If a joke falls flat when you are picking up a cake at a bakery, who cares? How likely are you to see the baker again?

The benefits of laughter—it increases retention (making you more memorable), it inspires agreement, it positions the *laugh maker* higher on the social ladder, and causes people to seek you out for more interaction—greatly outweigh the discomfort of striking out a few times when working on your humor skills. And if you think that humor is something you are either born with, or not, guess again. No one comes out of the womb with comedy skills. Even the greatest comedians spent years bombing before hitting their stride. The reason we think people are naturally funny is that the public isn't treated to Comedy Central specials of famous comedians *tanking* (comedian-speak for dying on stage). When Jerry Seinfeld ended the run of the *Seinfeld* sitcom, he decided to go back to touring as a stand-up comedian. The movie, *Comedian*, chronicles his post-sitcom journey back to stand-up. The challenge for Seinfeld was, he couldn't use any of his old material. The documentary follows him as he tries out new material (called *bits*) at comedy clubs across the country. Watching a seasoned pro like Seinfeld bomb while testing out new bits is all the proof you need to know that humor is a muscle, and everyone needs to keep exercising.

When I am practicing turning transactional relationships into connected ones, I add humor whenever possible. I was at a Target store buying batteries. All I had was one small package of AA batteries, so I stood in the *Ten Items or Less* aisle (behind everyone who had thirty items in their cart). Side note: The sign should read *Ten Items or Fewer*, not *Less*, but Americans stopped caring about grammar at about the same time they stopped wearing corsets. Be that as it may, while the young lady at the check-out counter was scanning each item from people's carts she would ask, "Do you want a bag?" "Do you want a bag?" "Do you want a bag?" She was *in the zone*. She scanned items with the speed of a Major League pitcher's fast ball, tossing items in the plastic bags that will still be on Earth long after humans have died off (from using too many plastic bags), and repeating, "Do you want a bag?" "Do you want a bag?" "Do you want a bag?"

It is when people are *in the zone* that you get the best practice at converting a transactional relationship to a connected one. The challenge is even greater because you have to do it without taking too much time. After all, there is a line of people behind you with thirty items in their cart. When it was my turn, she grabbed my tiny package of batteries off the conveyor belt, scanned it, and asked, "Do you want a bag?" I replied, "No, but I will need help carrying it to my car." Like a robot that had been suddenly switched off, her speedy motions came to a halt. She looked at the batteries, looked at me, looked at the batteries (smoke now coming out of her ears), and finally laughed and said, "Oh, cut it out!"

If you can get a laugh out of someone who is being paid minimum wage and forced to wear a vest that is red enough to flag down airliners, no measly networking function will frighten you. And it is no small feeling to know that you might be the one customer who brought laughter to someone's day. I use phone calls as practice as well, largely because the challenge is greater. Not having the visual cues upon which the brain relies in order to judge conversation, phone conversations add an extra element to the training. When my office phone rang one day and the Caller ID listed the name of a client, John Dee, I answered with, "Hello. John Dee Fan Club." John laughed, and I became such a memorable part of his day that, when we had a conference call later that week with a larger group, he said, "Everyone, this is Stevie Ray on the phone with us. And he is the president of my fan club!"

These might seem like small gestures, but they pay big dividends in keeping your skills sharp for the moment of truth, and for giving you that extra edge that could mean the difference between the job going to you or your evil competition.

One final word about not ignoring any possibility. I was conducting a workshop for a library association. Even though I try to turn every opportunity into more opportunities, I thought "What can a bunch of librarians do to grow my business?" Of course, I always put forth my best effort for every client; it's just that, in this case, I didn't expect any referral business. After the workshop, a number of librarians approached me with "My husband works at US Bank and his department would love this" and "My best friend is a manager at a department store and her staff would really appreciate these skills." They all asked for my business card, and I walked away with a good lesson about staying open to all possibilities.

CHAPTER 3

Do This, Don't Do That

If you are like most people, you skipped to this chapter as soon as you opened the book, thinking, "Let's see how I botched my last networking event." If you did, you committed mistake number one.

Don't Do This: Judge yourself negatively. In uncomfortable situations, people often think they are doing something wrong. A woman in one of my workshops was participating in a group exercise. Each time she spoke, she followed with a quick, "I'm sorry." I asked her why she kept apologizing and she said, "I'm not sure if I'm doing this exercise right." Her uncertainty about whether she was doing things right led her to assume she must be doing things wrong. She kept looking to others to reassure her, which made her appear weak.

It is easy to criticize the woman for lacking confidence, but there is a neurological basis for her apprehension, and it is a common challenge for all humans. If you recall from way back to page seven of this book (I know, it's a stretch), the default running mechanism of the brain is to provide safety for the host; or, more accurately, to avoid danger.

Because the brain has spent most of its evolutionary life being on the look-out for danger, it has developed a specific way to view sensory input. Whatever we experience through our eyes or ears will be judged as *safe* or *unsafe*. Because *unsafe* is more important, the brain is affected more strongly by negative input, and can hang onto the memory of bad experiences longer.

The result of this evolutionary attention to danger is that the brain is wired with twice as many receptors for negative input than for positive input. If someone pays you a compliment, "Hey, your presentation today was really impressive", quite often your response is to downplay your achievement, "Thanks, but I think I used too many PowerPoint slides." (Hint: If you ever have to ask yourself if you used too many PowerPoint slides, the answer is *probably yes*. If you don't ask yourself if you used too many slides, the answer is *definitely yes*.) Many people downplay compliments due to a few reasons: 1) you were are raised to value humility, 2) you know the presentation really did suck, 3) you are Lutheran, 4) the positive input receptors in your brain are being over-shadowed by the negative receptors. On the other hand, criticism gets free brain-reign. Whereas a compliment is often forgotten within a short time, a critique will stick in our brains for days.

Obviously, this condition doesn't apply to everyone, or affect everyone to the same degree. And the brain can be re-wired throughout your entire life, based on whether you choose to let your brain rule you, or the other way around. People can make a conscious choice to allow compliments to wash over themselves like a warm shower, and carry the positive effect of the compliment for days. These people typically outperform others. A brain that is in a positive state of mind thinks faster and more creatively. So, if you routinely deny compliments and obsess over critiques, make it a conscious effort to reverse that pattern.

These thought processes are the purview of the part of the brain called the *amygdala*. The amygdala controls base reactions—fear, rage, lust, and panic—while the higher centers of the brain, including the *dorsolateral prefrontal cortex*, controls what is called *executive function* such as, analysis, decision making, and choosing to stay on shore while your buddies try waterskiing with a trash can lid. Here is a tidbit about the amygdala that is worth knowing. Because women have traditionally been responsible for child-rearing, and men have been responsible for hunting, the amygdala reacts differently in male versus female brains. In order to raise children and keep them safe from harm, the female amygdala developed a reaction to sensory input that is much stronger than the male amygdala.

If a situation causes anger, panic, or fear, the female brain will react twice as strongly, and the reaction will last twice as long. Men, being traditionally responsible for hunting, have a suppressed amygdala response. If someone is waiting patiently for prey to appear, any distraction could mean no dinner, so the male brain is more adept at singular focus, while the female brain is more adept at managing multiple inputs, namely children. Remember the last time you were in a tense situation with a member of the opposite sex? Because the male amygdala response dissipates faster, a man can assume a woman is over-reacting to a situation. Whereas women can assume that men are uncaring. Neither accusation is always true, or false, but it is worth keeping in mind that female and male brains are wired to react differently, based on evolution.

This is, or course, a broad-brush description, and there are people who behave more like the opposite sex, and people who are considered *balanced brains*, but the reason for discussing all this brain stuff is to be aware that we can over-react while networking, and we can misjudge our own abilities. And our misjudgment can likely be negative without being justified. But before you dismiss Rule #1 and think, "My confidence level is fine," remember that most of our reactions are subconscious and take effort to manage. You may be sending negative signals without even knowing it.

I like to follow a rule, *always assume that, whatever you are doing, you are doing it correctly until told otherwise. And, if someone tells you that you are doing it wrong ask, "How do you know?"* If you are too harsh on yourself, your lack of self-confidence will show in your behavior. This makes you less desirable to work with. Not only do you enjoy networking less, but you don't get the job.

Don't Do This: Do all the talking. Marshall, an old friend of mine, is a consummate salesman. Whatever he is selling, or whichever company he is working for, he achieves Salesman of the Year status every year. As you might expect, Marshall is constantly being asked by less successful sales professionals for his big secret to success. He tells them, "You can never *talk* anybody into anything, but you can *listen* them into it." Marshall told me that he spends the majority of *sits* just listening. He knows that the more someone else talks, the more likely they are to buy. It is a psychological principle that, when allowed to talk, people more easily switch from a defensive position to a cooperative one.

The principle of listening to enhance cooperation is often used by police when interrogating a suspect. I attended a lecture by a police chief who said that, while they will sometimes (but rarely), use the hard-hitting interrogation tactics you see on *Law & Order*, they prefer a more nuanced, and effective, technique. The police chief said, "I will usually just go into the interrogation room and bring a bunch of paper work. I won't say a word to the *perp*, I'll just sit and fill out forms. After a long silence, and the perp getting more and more uncomfortable, he will finally say something like 'This is stupid. This is total B.S.' I won't respond with anything more than 'Oh really?' or 'Uh huh,' then I go right back to my paper work.

"After more silence, the guy will say, 'I didn't have anything to do with the store getting knocked off. I wasn't even there.' After more silence, 'Well, I wasn't there, but I was close. But I didn't even know the guys who did it…okay, except my brother.' If I sit silent long enough, he will give me the whole story." You can probably guess that the police chief isn't invited to a lot of parties. Of course, the entire process is more complicated than this story, and I don't introduce this technique in the hopes that you will network by sitting silently and staring at the other person. I mention it because the quickest path to building trust is to listen. I was going to add that it is also the easiest path, but if you are like me, sitting with your mouth shut is far from easy.

We trust people who allow us to vent. We judge them to be more caring and intelligent. The ability to listen is also considered to be a sign of intelligence; talking often proves the opposite. I had a friend, Jim, visit me from out of town on the day I was to attend a party. He didn't know anyone at the party, but I didn't want to leave him sitting in his hotel room so I invited him along. When we arrived at the party he said, "I don't want to shadow you the whole time, so you hang out with your friends and I'll catch up with you at the end of the night."

At the end of the party people came up to me and asked, "Who is that Jim that you brought with you? He is a fascinating person!" I always considered Jim to be a regular guy, so I was anxious to find out his technique for wowing people at the party. As soon as we left the party I asked, "What did you say to everyone to make them think you were so fascinating?" He said, "Oh, I knew that I wouldn't know anyone at the party, and wasn't likely going to see any of them again, so I didn't want to spend the night repeating all the same stuff about myself. So I decided not to talk about myself once throughout the entire night. I just kept asking people questions about themselves. The funny thing is, I didn't say a word about myself, yet they thought I was the most interesting person they had ever met." If this had been a networking event, everyone would have asked for Jim's business card.

To develop your own listening skills, try an exercise called *Five Minute Conversation*. Sit with a friend and have her talk about herself for five minutes. She should talk about herself, not about the weather or politics. As the listener, you are not allowed to say a word for the entire five minutes. You may look interested (nod your head, smile), but you can't say anything. At the end of the five minutes, you must tell your partner everything you can remember about what she said. Switch places a few times and see how your skills improve with practice.

This exercise can be challenging for both parties. For some people, talking about themselves for that long without verbal feedback is very uncomfortable. This is because we aren't socialized to talk without being interrupted. A good deal of conversation involves using the verbal and nonverbal cues from our partner to signal which direction to take the conversation. As such, this exercise is good practice for keeping a listener engaged; keeping them hooked. Keeping someone engaged means you must develop passion for what you are talking about. During the exercise, you must avoid phrases like, "Oh, let's see. What else can I tell you about myself?" You must instead focus on making your story, and yourself, fascinating. If you think your life is dull, other people will too. How fascinating you are has little to do with the *coolness* of your life experiences; it has to do with how much life you bring to the everyday things you do.

Another difficult part of the exercise is having to listen without speaking for five whole minutes. When people are engaged in conversation, they want to comment on things that they find interesting. This is especially true when the other person describes a situation that also happened to us. Being social creatures, humans love to share common experiences. This is great for bonding. However, if you jump too quickly on someone else's story with your own experience, it can ruin networking. You will be judged as self-centered, selfish, and less intelligent.

Advising you to make your story, and yourself, interesting may seem contradictory to the earlier rule of listening to others and focusing on their story. However, good conversation is a balance of listening and talking. Conversation is like playing catch with a ball. When your partner throws you the ball, it is your turn to have it. When it is the other person's turn, you throw the ball back. A game of catch doesn't work if you hang onto the ball the entire time. Good networking is like a good game of catch.

Don't Do This: Ask before offering. I mentioned this mistake earlier in the book. Blurting out your *ask*, "Hey, I'm looking for someone who needs printing services, let me give you my card just in case." is one of the quickest ways to send your prospect running to the door. If you appear needy, you won't get the job even if you are perfect for the position.

I once attended a new-member event at an association. If you have ever been invited to a member-recruitment event, you know the kind of pressure to which the guests are subjected. These *bring a friend* events rarely work. If current members truly believed in the worth of the organization, they should be talking up its benefits whenever they meet someone who they think would be a good fit. Forcing members to scroll through their database to fulfill the obligation of bringing a guest is never comfortable. And the event itself never ends up showcasing the organization in the best light. Throughout the evening, current members circulate around the room welcoming the strangers, talking about how wonderful the organization is and saying, "It would be great to have you as a member." Guests feel like gazelles surrounded by hungry hyenas. If anyone does join the organization, it is either because they had decided to join before they attended the meeting, or because they didn't want to say no to their host.

When I arrived at the event, I decided I wasn't going to pressure anyone into joining the association. In fact, I decided that I wasn't going to talk about the organization that was hosting the event at all. My challenge was, whoever I met that night, I would dig for any problems they were experiencing and offer solutions to help their business. I am good at brainstorming new ideas. My reasoning was, if I could be of service to any guest here, they would see the value of joining the organization without me pushing them into it.

Shortly after the event began, I met a young couple who looked like the gazelles I spoke of. They sat in a corner of the room with their appetizer-sized plates of crab cakes and meat-on-a-skewer. Nothing gives people the feeling of confidence like having to balance messy foods on your lap while holding an over-priced drink in your hand. I approached and introduced myself. It was clear that Barry and Jen weren't going to mingle on their own, and they were young enough that these types of events were not familiar territory, so, at first, I kept the conversation away from business. For some people, getting right to business is preferable to small-talk, but it was obvious that this conversation would be best handled with a lighter touch. After getting to know each other a bit, I asked what they did, and they owned and operated a photography studio. Barry was the photographer and Jen was the business manager.

I asked how business was going for them and they said, "Fine." This is typical. If you ask anyone how things are going, the initial response is usually, "Fine." The trick is to not let that be the end of it; moving on to sports or the weather. Networking requires digging for people's pain and seeing if your company can be the one to solve it. So you have to get past *fine* and discover what is really going on. So I asked question after question, *How do you find your clients? Are you keeping your calendar full? Are you getting as many referrals as you like?* If you let people talk, especially about their business, their problems will emerge. Remember the *Five Minute Conversation* exercise? It is not an easy exercise to put into practice. Every time Barry and

Jen brought up a new problem, I wanted to cut in and relate it to something I had experienced. But this conversation wasn't supposed to be about me, so I kept my own stories to myself.

It wasn't long before Jen and Barry started telling me about how challenging it was to compete with larger franchises. About how repeat clients were tough to establish. About how some customers were nearly impossible to satisfy. And the most difficult problem, and the reason they probably came to the association event that night, how they just couldn't get the word out about their business because they didn't have a budget for advertising.

Here is where networking and socializing take different forks in the road. If a friend or family member vents about their frustrations, they usually just want you to listen. They don't want you to solve their problems, they just want a sympathetic ear. If married men could learn this one simple lesson, there would be fewer couches being used as beds for the night. Without getting into the psychology of male and female brains, men's brains are wired to solve problems. It is almost impossible for us to hear a problem without saying, "Well, why don't you just do this and everything would be fine?" I have had some guys in my workshops who couldn't try *Five Minute Conversation* without talking after the first minute.

In networking, however, good business owners and professionals are eager to hear any new ideas you can offer. A sympathetic ear is fine, but a money-making idea or a solution to a problem is what we are looking for. So, every time Jen and Barry commiserated about a problem at the photography studio, I offered some solutions. And I didn't just say, "You should try this," I made sure they felt they weren't alone in the solution. It is easy to simply tell someone what to do, but giving them a partner in the solution carries more power. For each solution I offered, I added, "Mr. Jones is a member of this association and he does that kind of thing a lot. I'll introduce you so he can tell you how to do it at your studio." Instead of a hyena looking for a meal, I became a of source of solutions for Barry and Jen's problems. By the end of the night, they were asking about how to join the association. And I never once brought up membership during the conversation.

Don't Do This: Skip your homework. Bad economies seem to beget bad networking. People are so desperate for business that they do things that hurt instead of help. In 2007, when the Great Recession was beginning to hit, I received a call at my office:

"Hello, Stevie Ray's Improv Company."
"Is Stevie Ray available?"
"This is he."
"Hi Mr. Ray, this is Becky Turnquist at *The Big Bank*. I am calling to talk about having our bank help your company with its financial needs."
"Thanks, but we're pretty happy with our bank."
"Okay. May I ask who you bank with currently?"
"No, thank you. Thanks for calling."

"Thank you, Mr. Ray. Have a nice day."

The Big Bank probably had that woman sitting on the phone calling dozens of companies every day. And I would be astonished if it resulted in any new business. The first mistake was waiting for things to get tough at the bank before calling me. Business people can tell when we are a desperation call. More importantly, however, was the fact that the woman didn't make any real connection between our two companies before asking for my business. Her call made me feel insulted, rather than flattered. I ended up feeling worse about their bank than if they hadn't called me at all. At least with no contact from them I wouldn't assume they were lazy. What if that woman had done just a little homework before calling me?

"Hello, Stevie Ray's Improv Company"
"Hi, this is Becky Turnquist from *The Big Bank*, is Stevie Ray available?"
"This is he."
"Hello Mr. Ray. I'm in charge of small business development here at *The Big Bank*. I've been looking into your company to see if we might be a good fit for your business. From what I have been able to learn, I see that you offer entertainment as well as corporate training. That seems to be a very unique combination of services."
"Yes, we do have a unique business model…"

At this point, if the caller is smart, she would let me continue talking about my business. The longer I talk, the more I trust her. After I finish, she continues with,

"That's a really interesting business approach. If you don't mind me asking, how do you keep the two branches separate, but still market them under one company name?"

Now is when she is likely to hear about our problems. After I vent for a while, she suggests...

"Mr. Ray, we have worked with a lot of companies that are about your size and industry. We have discovered that companies like yours typically make five mistakes in their banking that cost them money. I'm calling businesses like yours to make sure that they don't make those mistakes, especially now when losing any amount of money can cripple a business. I would love to set up a twenty-minute meeting and give you this information. Now, even though I think our bank would be a great fit for you, I promise not to try to sell you anything at the meeting. It would just be an informational meeting. If you find it valuable and want to do business together after that, then we could talk about possibilities. If that sounds good to you, let's take a look at our calendars."

To be sure, this approach doesn't make people drop everything they're doing and rush to meet you, but showing the respect of learning about the other person and their company means you are responsible, intelligent, and take initiative. Those are the kinds of people with whom we want to do business. Obviously, you can't do background homework on people you might meet at an event. So, since you don't have the opportunity to learn about a prospect before the event, ask a lot of questions during the meeting. Networking is like dating, if you don't show a keen interest in the other person; no second date.

Don't Do This: Not follow up. Barry and Jen left the meeting with all the membership applications and information they needed to join the association, but they never joined. It was my fault. I did a great job of connecting with them during the meeting (I am great at face-to-face), but I never followed up with them after the event (I suck at follow-up). If I had taken the time to make a couple of quick phone calls, our relationship would have been cemented. I made the mistake of thinking, "If they are interested, they will call."

Good follow-up contains two crucial elements: 1) consistency, 2) benefit. My company offers weekly classes to the public. The skills we teach are based on improvisation, or improv, but they are focused on helping people improve skills for work and life, not just for stage performance. To get new students, we placed an advertisement in a local newspaper every week for about fifteen years. As you can imagine, that newspaper loved us. We were the best kind of advertisers a newspaper could want, they never had to call us to renew the ad, and we sent a check every month. One year we noticed that the ad was no longer producing results, so we cancelled our account.

All of a sudden the newspaper realized that we weren't such a *sure thing* anymore. We were like the girlfriend that was neglected once too often. Once we said, "I want to start dating other people," the advertising manager wanted to know what he could do to keep dating. You should have seen the hoops he was willing to jump through to get us back; enhancing our ad with color, special placement on the page, etc. It was, of course, too late. We had started dating other people. Then he started the follow up calls. Once a month I would get a phone call:

"Hello, Stevie Ray's Improv Company."
"Stevie?"
"Yes."
"Hi. It's Mitch from *The Big Newspaper*. Just calling to see if you have any advertising needs we can help with."
"No, we're fine. Thanks anyway."
"Okay, have a nice day."

Those calls came in steadily for about three years after we closed our account. Then he finally got the hint and we haven't heard from him since. Even though the calls were consistent, they never resulted in the newspaper getting our business because the call was all about them and not about us. Frankly, my business partner and I were even more insulted after the fact. Notice that the extras he offered us—colored ink, special placement—came only after we told them we were leaving. Shouldn't a valued client of fifteen years get those perks as a thank-you? Not as a desperate attempt to save the relationship?

If you make a connection, keep it strong by *giving something* to the person frequently. Send an article that you think they would find interesting, or a bit of news about their industry. Offer to do something to help their business with no request for a return favor. Gifts are reciprocated down the road. Even simple day-brighteners are seen as gifts; funny ads you spot in a newspaper or a comic strip you can forward by e-mail. The tradition in sales was to make contact once a month, but new research has shown that communication like this should be frequent, but spontaneous. If communication has a clockwork feel to it, it loses its impact. Make these *touches* spontaneous, surprising, and something that will have your prospect smiling when he or she thinks of you.

Don't Do This: Rely On Your Business Card. Many people think that getting their business card into someone's hand constitutes networking. Remember Susie Johnson from the networking event that flitted from person to person shoving her business card in their hands? Hunters call this *scatter-shooting*, blasting a shotgun with as wide a pattern of buckshot as possible in the hopes that one of them will hit something. (In the old West, shotguns were called *scatter* guns.) There is about as much luck hunting with the *scatter-shoot* method as there is in networking.

However ineffective it is, many people rely on the, "Let me give you my card" tactic. Like most people, I don't like to deny someone face-to-face, so I'll take their card. As soon as I hit my office, their card hits the trash. I finally realized that if I'm throwing away business cards because I didn't ask for them, the same is likely happening to mine if I shove them into people's hands. Now I now follow a strict rule, *I never give my business card to anyone unless they ask for it.* This means I must make myself so valuable that they need my card. The way to make sure of this is simple; if you spend your time talking mostly about what you do and how great it is, it isn't likely that people will want your card. However, if you discuss the other person's needs and challenges, and offer solutions to their problems, you will be seen as a valuable resource. Your business card will no longer be a polite exchange of pleasantries, to be forgotten as soon as the evening is over; but a tool to make their life easier and more profitable.

Don't Do This: Look for a job/client/prospect. I had an acquaintance, Anne, who was finishing graduate school and making plans to go out into the real world. She was nervous because the market was tight and she wasn't sure if companies were hiring people with her specific qualifications. We met for lunch, but I didn't ask her about her college degree or what she was qualified to do. Instead I asked her what she thought were her core talents. I asked her, "If you didn't have to worry about making a living, what would you do for free?" Anne responded the way most people do when talking about something as intangible as talent, she listed off the things she liked to do and followed each one with, "but who's going to give me a job doing that?"

Americans have spent so many years defining ourselves by the positions we hold that we often miss the big picture. This limits our ability to position ourselves in the market place correctly. We see ourselves as the *takers* looking for help from the *givers*. Instead of looking for ways to best use our talents, we look for a job opening, a new client, or a new piece of business. Instead of wondering who could benefit from our skills, we wonder who will buy us.

During my meeting with Anne, I got her thinking, not about what kind of job she might get, but what kind of service she could provide. I explained, "If you ask someone if they have any job openings or are looking to hire someone, the answer is almost always 'No.' Asking for a job, or seeking a new client, puts the other person in the position of satisfying your needs and solving your problems. Instead, you have to be seen as a person who will solve theirs. Talking about your core talents gets people thinking, 'Wow, I could sure use someone like that.' You shift from being a burden to a resource."

Once we shifted Anne's thinking, the rest was easy. She talked about the things she loved to do, the things that she was passionate about. The result was a shift in her attitude. Earlier, when she was talking only about what kind of job she might be able to get, she sounded needy and apprehensive. When she spoke about her talents and what she truly loved to do, she was alive and full of energy. Energetic people are much more hire-able. Great leaders know that putting together a great team involves more than knowing the qualifications of each individual team member.

Someone with Anne's passion and drive would be a great addition to any team.

Once we identified Anne's true talents, I sent an e-mail to my contact list, "Hello, Stevie Ray here. I have a friend, Anne, who has finished becoming really smart at graduate school and is now ready to use her skills to benefit the right company. Her talent is dealing with people face-to-face, explaining difficult concepts so they are easily understood, and getting people excited about trying new things. She is not so good at walking around with a clipboard making sure processes are being implemented. Instead, she thrives in an environment where she can offer new ideas to improve processes, especially when it deals with person-to-person interactions. Anne has traveled extensively, so she also thrives being on the road or dealing with a multi-cultural environment. Please look around your organization and see if you have a need for someone with Anne's skills."

Notice what I left out of the e-mail? No mention of a degree (although you know she has one because I mentioned her finishing graduate school). Also, no mention of what position she was looking for. If you ask, "Do you need anyone with IT experience?" the person would mentally scroll through her roster of IT people and decide yes or no. This leaves little room for thinking creatively about how an organization might benefit from someone's unique skills.

Because my e-mail told people what Anne could do for them, they started thinking about all the places they could use her. With the talents I listed, she could be a trainer, salesperson, HR professional, customer service representative, or regional manager. She received responses the very next day stating, "I think we have something that Anne would be perfect for. I'll have the head of the department contact her."

I have another friend named Kat. She was getting restless at her old job and wanted a change. Kat is not one to sit around and wait for an opportunity to be handed to her. She decided that she wanted to work for one of the largest advertising companies in the region, but the job she wanted didn't exist at the company. She called the company and said, "I know you don't currently have this position in your company, but creating it would serve your clients better and make things run more smoothly." After the company got over the shock of being told they were missing a position they never knew existed, they agreed and asked her to be patient for a year so they could create it for her. She now runs the new department with a support staff of her own.

PART II

Working the Room

Now for the real nitty gritty. There you are, a small plate of appetizers in one hand, a drink in the other, surrounded by a roomful of professionals all dressed up. It's time to shake hands, introduce yourself, and get some business. Remember what we talked about at the beginning of the book; there is a big difference between networking and socializing. This is where you realize why the majority of business is still closed by face-to-face networking rather than electronic communication. You can tell everything you need to know about a person by looking him or her in the eye.

In his book, *Social Intelligence*, Daniel Goldman talks about connections between people that occur at the most basic, neurological level. Being social creatures, humans have evolved with the ability to discern subtle cues about each other during conversation. These signals are such a basic part of our neural make-up that we are largely unaware of them. When we say we have a *gut feeling* about someone, it comes from the neural network that determines whether we should trust this new person. This is the

Approach/Withdraw Response discussed earlier in the book. And, you might recall, our intellect often overrides this neural, gut feeling. We talk ourselves out of trusting our instincts, later resulting in the, "I wish I had listened to my gut in the first place" feeling.

Networking is the chance for you to make the kind of connections where people like you, trust you, and want to work with you so badly that they will make excuses, create positions, and shift budgets to do so. Unfortunately, you can also turn a networking opportunity into the perfect place to show the world what a doofus you are.

I was conducting a training session for a law firm that I had worked with often over the years. This is a large firm; they typically hire 50-60 new attorneys every year. As part of their week-long orientation, where they would learn policies and procedures, I would conduct a workshop on effective client communication skills. A few days before my workshop, the director of training called and said, "I know you usually do pretty high-level stuff for us, but I need you to dumb it down a bit this year." You don't hear that kind of request very often, especially when dealing with lawyers, so he had my full attention. He continued, "The kids coming out of law school these days are graduating with far fewer social skills than ever before. Young women are arriving for work wearing outfits that are far too revealing and provocative. The guys are showing up wearing fashions that you see in hip-hop stores.

"Stevie, here is the situation. We are a well-respected firm. We routinely win business away from firms in the biggest cities in the country, which isn't easy because these big clients often assume that we are a bunch of hayseeds because we aren't located in New York or Los Angeles. We consider taking clients away from those markets a big win for the firm. Quite often, the other partners of the firm and I will be out of the office when a valued client hits town unexpectedly. When they are in town, they think, "Let's stop in at our firm of record and take a look around. So they stop in for a surprise visit. We have to trust that our new associates can be the *face of the firm* and escort our clients around the building, take them to lunch, and impress them. With the social skills these associates have now, we are afraid that the client will think 'I guess these guys are the hicks we thought they were,' and pull their account. And we have seen this happen, so the threat is real. You have to help us set these new attorneys up for success; for the sake of themselves, and the firm."

I empathized with the training director. I am all for freedom of expression and I think quite a few companies could stand to loosen up their dress codes a bit, but your appearance has to represent what you sell. And the text-instead-of-talk environment that has taken over the world has severely hampered the development of crucial social skills. Texting can't teach you what you need to know for face-to-face interaction. And face-to-face is where we live.

I asked my friend, Gary, to help create a workshop designed to help these attorneys understand why certain signals can turn off a prospective client. You might find this approach valuable for your organization. We had all the lawyers sit at tables of eight people. Everyone was given a pad of paper and a pen. We told them that Gary and I were going to play out a typical networking scenario, a firm-sponsored social event with clients as guests. Gary would be playing the part of a valued client attending the function, and I would play the part of a lawyer from the firm. We told them that there were a number of pre-planned faux pas I would commit, and that they were to write down as many as they spotted. After the scenario was finished, each table would confer and create a master list of mistakes and we would compare the lists to see which table detected the most networking mistakes.

During the scene, I made every mistake I could think of. I didn't stand when Gary approached my table. I motioned for him to sit while I remained seated. I crossed my legs cross-wise instead of at the knee. And when I crossed my legs, I had socks that were too short so I flashed some leg skin. I garishly waved across the room to an imaginary server for another drink. When the server arrived, I ordered for myself without first offering Gary something to drink. In fact, I didn't ask him if he wanted anything at all. I called across the room to an acquaintance while Gary was talking. My body language displayed arrogance and lack of interest. When he asked about a service related to my firm I told him to give us a call the next day rather than offering to call him. In all, I figured I had made about two dozen faux pas.

These social fumbles might seem obvious, but they are based on mistakes I see committed at every networking session I attend. When we finished our scenario, we asked the tables to confer. People love a bit of friendly competition, so we told them we were going to see which table caught the most mistakes and offer a prize for the winning table. Not surprisingly, tables with mainly younger, inexperienced staff members didn't catch as many mistakes as tables that had seasoned veterans. The younger lawyers caught about twelve mistakes. The table with a senior partner caught thirty-seven! I asked for the senior partner's list immediately after the workshop.

Working the room doesn't just mean shaking everyone's hand and smiling. It means entering conversations smoothly, exiting at the right time, listening when it's your turn and talking when it's your turn. Some of these skills seem natural, but they don't develop without paying attention to them.

First, let's start with how you introduce yourself.

CHAPTER 4

"So, What Do You Do?"

In Latin American and Asian countries, it is "Tell me about your family." In Scandinavian countries, "What is your hobby?" In the Middle East, it could include all of the above, along with "How is your health? How is your family's health?" And all might add a dose of, "Where are you from?" In the U.S., where we kneel at the altar of the Almighty Profession, it's "So, what do you do?" It is, in fact, considered rude in many countries to jump straight to inquiring about one's work. Such a misstep is viewed as placing more importance on someone's job than the person's life. Regardless of the ever-flattening planet upon which we live, it is good to have an engaging response to "So, what do you do?" Sadly, most people have a terribly un-engaging response.

I was at a chamber of commerce luncheon with approximately fifty attendees. At the start of the meeting, each member stood up and said his or her name, place of business, and a short pitch about their company. Rather than focus on each person's introduction, I paid close attention to the group that was listening; gauging whether they were truly interested in the person's pitch. I observed two things;

1) most introductions were terrible, 2) hardly anyone paid attention during the introductions. Everyone was just waiting for their turn to speak. This got me to wondering, how do you capture someone's attention when you know their chief motivation for being there is to promote themselves? It starts with what you say about yourself.

The reason most introductions fail to achieve their goal—to engage the listener, encourage further contact, gain business, and inspire referrals—is because of one of the worst practices to ever be adopted by professional networking: the *elevator pitch*. If you are unfamiliar with the practice, an elevator pitch calls for you to have a planned introduction that will capture the attention of a prospect in the shortest amount of time, such as during a chance meeting in an elevator. The elevator pitch concept is accurate in only one of its assumptions; that you have only a short period of time in which to spark the interest of a prospect. This is true whether your actual face-time is short, as in an elevator ride, or if you are having an extended conversation over dinner. If you don't capture someone's attention quickly, they will mentally check out, even if they seem like they are listening intently about the time you caught a twenty-two-pound largemouth bass out of Lake Michigan using a dried-up Cheeto for bait.

Having a planned, canned, introduction is wrong on many levels. I will explain using a real-life example. At one of my networking workshops, I had everyone sit at tables of eight people. I had everyone take turns introducing themselves to their table guests. When everyone was finished, I said, "Point to the person whose introduction you remember most." Once they all pointed to someone, I continued with, "If three or more people are pointing at you, stand up." Only a few people stood. I then asked the people who had pointed at the *winners*, what they remembered about the introductions. Every time I play this game, the answer to this question is the same, "He made me laugh," "I was surprised by some tidbit about her life," or "I don't know. She just stood out from the rest." People never point at someone who simply described their company or their job.

The people who had others pointing at them will get work because they have overcome the first hurdle in networking, being memorable. As we discussed earlier in the book, memory is affected by primacy, frequency, and urgency. We can't affect primacy or frequency, but we can affect how urgent the listener wants to engage with us. Urgency doesn't always refer to the weightiness of our offering, the brain will also consider someone an urgent connection if that person is fun to be around, or is unique.

If you use a pre-planned elevator pitch—replying to every "So, what do you do?" with the same response—you lose the spontaneity and humor that drives people to connect. Elevator pitches also fail to achieve another crucial outcome of good networking; they fail to solve the needs of the listener. The most effective way to keep people interested in you is to become a resource for solving their problems. No one ever really goes out in search of a marketing expert, but they do go out in search of someone who can help solve the problem of *How do customers find me?* We discussed this earlier while looking at Robert Middleton's concept of talking about the pain you solve, rather than the good you provide. This goes along with the psychological guideline; *people move more quickly away from pain than they do toward pleasure.* Because the elevator pitch is pre-planned, it completely ignores the unique needs of each individual you might meet while networking.

I demonstrate this to groups by having someone stand in the room as if he were at a networking event. I tell the group that I'm going to approach the guy and ask, "So, what do you do?" The group's job is to watch me approach the man and, based on my attitude, determine what I need. They are not to determine what I need in terms of what service I am looking for, or what issues I might have, but what I need from my partner in order to make the interaction comfortable.

The first time I approach the man, I act very shy and timid. I ask, "Uh…so, what do you do?" At this point, I stop and ask the group, "What do I need?" Most shout, "More self-confidence!" Those who respond this way aren't thinking of serving me, they are judging me. They judged me as inadequate. As such, their ability to connect with me will be hampered. People can sense when they have been judged. Others in the group respond with, "You need your partner to make you feel comfortable" or "You need your partner to carry the weight of the conversation." Bingo. If you think in terms of "how can I give this person what he needs?" you will avoid judging others.

When I play this game, I approach the man with many different attitudes; blustery, frustrated, chatty, bored, high-powered business type, etc. People who understand the concept of making your partner comfortable recognize that the frustrated man needs someone who will let him vent, the chatty one needs a partner who will chat, the self-important man needs someone who will let him talk.

Rather than judge any of these emotions as positive or negative, a good networker sees them as clues as to how to best serve a prospect. If every person needs something different from you, how can you possibly use the same introduction, or elevator pitch, for all of them? Some people need you to be reassuring, others need you to be high-powered and exciting, while others need you to get to the point.

I teach an exercise in my workshops called, "So, what do you do?" A group of people sit in a circle. One person stands up and faces the person to her left, who asks, "So, what do you do?" The introducer answers, then faces the next person in the circle, who also asks, "What do you do?" She continues until she has introduced herself to each person in the circle.

The game seems simple until you add an important qualifier, the *introducer* is not allowed to use the same introduction twice. He or she must use a different introduction for each person in the circle. You should see the sweat break out on people's faces after they have used up their canned pitch. People get so accustomed to describing themselves the same way that breaking the pattern is next to impossible. You may think that you have an effective introduction because you have developed a succinct way to describe yourself, but the very fact that you use the same introduction in every scenario sets you up for failure. After playing this game, people realize just how much of a crutch their elevator pitch has become. This illuminates a key failing of the elevator pitch; it is designed to make the introduction easier for the person delivering it than for the person receiving it.

You might be wondering, "How do you know which approach will work for a person you have never met?" The answer comes from a course I took with the great Paul Sills. Sills was one of the founders of The Second City Theatre in Chicago. The Second City is known for sketch comedy similar the hit TV show, *Saturday Night Live*. In fact, *Saturday Night Live* gets most of its performers from The Second City. What many people don't know is that much of the sketch material at The Second City is developed using the techniques of improvisation, or *improv*.

When Sills was developing The Second City in the late '50s, he needed his troupe of performers to connect with each other quickly, form cohesive teams, create new and innovative work, and perform together smoothly. To do this, he used improv techniques developed by his mother, Viola Spolin. Viola Spolin was an educator and innovator who developed groundbreaking techniques to unlock people's potential. Much of her work is detailed in her book, *Improvisation for the Theatre*, but Spolin and Sills carried their techniques beyond the theatre and into the real world of communication and human interaction. Their work in improvisation spawned such TV shows as *Whose Line Is It Anyway?*

I attended a weeklong training camp with Sills when he was in his final years of teaching. A group of sixteen people from around the country were selected to learn classic improvisation. He started by saying, "We're going to practice improvisation now, but for Pete's sake don't make anything up!" We were understandably confused. We asked, "How can we improvise if we don't make anything up?" Sills replied, "You are not making anything up. It's already out there. The entire scene is already on the stage waiting for you to find it. It was created long before you got here. All you have to do is go out there and discover it."

The woman sitting next to me asked, "But, if we can't make anything up, how do we know what to say?" Sills responded, "You don't decide what to say. Your partner will tell you what to say. With every facial expression, every movement, and every word, your partner tells you what to say in order to make the scene work. All you have to do is listen. The problem is, no one really listens. They just wait to talk." A negative term in improvisation is *playwriting*. A playwright is someone who writes the entire script, then hands the script to actors. Since improvisation relies on the actors to cooperate in order to spontaneously create the scene, someone who plans ahead just how the scene will play out does not allow the full participation of his or her partners. Beginning improv students will playwright a lot because they are so nervous about where improv scenes will take them, and whether the scene will turn out well. This nervousness causes the student to force his or her ideas onto the other actors in order to control the outcome.

As you might guess, trying to improvise with someone who is playwriting is frustrating. Your own ideas are shoved to side in favor of his *better* ideas. Sills told our group that he would not be teaching us how to perform comedy improv, as seen on TV. Instead, he would focus on keeping us *in the moment*. Being *in the moment* means you are open to whatever your partner brings to the scene, and are able to adjust to the situation. The opposite of being *in the moment* is being *in your head*. Being *in your head* means you are overthinking the situation, worried about the outcome, and are at risk of playwrighting in an attempt to control the scene. Sills told us he would take us through a week of exercises and he would only criticize when he saw us *in our head* or playwrighting.

Sills was masterful at reading the thoughts of each member of the group. At one point, during an exercise where two members were having a particularly tough time, Sills stopped and said to one man, "Are you aware that we can all see you?" This startled the man, and confused the rest of us. Sills said, "You are so busy being in your head that you don't even know the rest of us exist. Why don't you just type out your script and mail it to your partner? That way you can make sure she doesn't screw up your well-laid plans." When it was my turn I thought, "I'm not going to make the same mistake as that guy." The funny thing is, by telling myself to avoid his mistake, I put myself *in my head*, making it impossible to be *in the moment* with my partner. A few minutes into the exercise, Paul stopped us and looked at me. "You're in your head, aren't you?" he asked. As much as I thought I was fully *in the moment*, I had to admit that I had lost focus. "Why are you in your head?" he asked. I replied, "Because I am worried about where we are going with this interaction." Sills said a great piece of advice, for improv and for life, "If you worry about where you are going, you will destroy where you are right now. You have this great partner ready to help you succeed, and you are ignoring her."

I have taken that advice into every networking session I have attended. If you listen, *really* listen, you never have to think of what to say. Your partner will tell you what to say in order to be successful. No pre-planned pitch can take the place of listening and being *in the moment*.

Be excited about yourself. No, this isn't an episode of *Dr. Phil* where I tell you that it is time to get excited about new possibilities. You would be surprised at how many people introduce themselves with a complete lack of enthusiasm; sometimes even an air of apology. I often hear people say "I'm just a..." The word *just* implies that your life is boring or inconsequential. At one event I heard a women say, "I'm just a teacher." *Just* a teacher? Let's see. She watches over 30 children in a room all day; a job that requires enough energy to power the city of Hong Kong for a week. She needed a graduate degree for her licensure, and must continually recertify and re-educate herself to meet ever-changing state and federal guidelines. She must engage and educate a roomful of brains that are so disparate they might as well be a UN Council. She is responsible for making sure the next generation is prepared to repair whatever mistakes the older generation has dumped on the planet. And for all this, she gets paid less than a Disc Jockey on an AM radio station in Juneau, Alaska. I love the slogan, *Those who can, teach. Those who can't teach, make laws about teaching.*

When we encounter people whose lives seem so much more exciting than our own, we feel the need to apologize for not having climbed Mount Everest or built a Fortune 500 company. Never apologize because you think that what you do doesn't measure up to others' accomplishments. Remember, people don't care what you do, they care about what you get done (for them). And they care about how much you care about what you do. Your job title is only a small part of your identity, and it is a woefully inadequate indication of who you are.

This is not to suggest that you act like a motivational speaker or preacher from the pulpit whenever you speak about what you do. False energy is just as much of a turn-off as uber-humility, but a key fact about the human brain to keep in mind is that we are classified by psychologists and social neuroscientists as being a *cued response animal*. This means that people aren't wired to collect information, analyze the information, and reach a logical conclusion. Instead, we engage in behavior based on cues that we get from those around us. Our socialness, the intricate link between the brains of a group, has been the advantage that has kept our weak species alive for millennia. The subconscious tendency to act according to group norms is a definite advantage when danger strikes the tribe.

The downside of being a *cued response animal* is that we can unknowingly cue others to reject us by engaging in behaviors that send the wrong signal. A simple shrug of the shoulders, shake of the head, or upturn of the palms—an *I'm not sure of myself* posture—essentially tells the listener not to trust what we say. Earlier in the book we discussed how the visual cortex is more powerful than the auditory cortex. It gathers and evaluates input more efficiently, and its interpretation always wins. However, if you gesture with weakness and then back up the gestures with words like *just* or *only*, you might as well pack up your business cards and head home.

Forget your title. When asked, "So, what do you do?" avoid relying too heavily on your job title to do the work of networking for you. Remember the people who were asked to stand at the networking workshop because their introductions were the most memorable? None of them were memorable because they said, "I'm a realtor." Most job titles are boring. One of the men at the workshop who was memorable introduced himself with, "Hi. I'm Jim. My proudest accomplishment is that I survived raising two teenaged daughters. That's my real life. For my living, I help make sure people have enough money to retire, even if they have two teenaged daughters." His introduction was not laugh-out-loud funny, but it displayed a nice sense of humor. Nowhere in his intro did Jim mention his job title. I met another man, Bill, at a conference. Bill was a financial advisor, but he never introduced himself as such. No one really wants to talk to a financial advisor, but we all want to be wealthy. Bill's business card read, "Bill Baxter, *Facilitator of Wealth*." He gets a lot of attention.

Of course, the risk here is that you can go too far and end up sounding phony. I have heard people try too hard to be interesting and say things like, "My name is Marcia, I help people dream big, and then reach out and achieve those dreams!" In Marcia's case, I would have preferred she skip the mini commercial. She also was too vague, leaving me wondering just which dreams she was talking about; retirement, wealth, fame, cool car, or good looks.

Networking requires rising above the mundane, yet avoiding the spurious. The easiest way to do that is to think, not about the tasks you perform, but what you love about your job. "I am a financial planner" sounds boring and typical. "I really love helping young people avoid the usual mistakes newly married couples make with their money" sounds genuine and interesting. The second statement will spur more responses of "How do you do that?" than the first. And, surprisingly, the more you narrow the definition of what you love to do, the more people outside of that definition will be interested in working with you. Rather than cutting off possibilities by using a narrow description, you open the door for more.

Make the other person ask, "How do you do that?" Have you ever listened to someone introduce themselves and thought, "That's nice. Where's the buffet?" Your introduction should inspire people to want to know more about you. When Jim said, "I help people save enough money to retire, even if they have two teenaged daughters," he described the exact problem that he helps solve. If he had just said that he helps people save money for retirement, we would think, "Oh. You're a financial planner. Boring." We would then put him in the same part of our brain as every other financial planner. Not only are we not interested, but we think, "I don't need that."

Adding a problem or challenge to an introduction makes us curious as to how you solve it. When Jim says that he can help us save money, even in the face of two credit-card carrying daughters, we want to know his secret. We wonder, "How do you do that?" If you can get people to ask "How do you do that?" after your introduction, you have them hooked.

I used to tell people, "I teach communication skills." That got me vacant stares. Now I say, "I help people deal with other people, especially when those other people aren't easy to deal with," to which they respond, "How do you do that?" However, I am careful to follow the advice from earlier. I make sure not to use that phrase every time I introduce myself. Doing so would make it hackneyed and stale. It would also prevent me from introducing myself in a way that best fits the person I'm speaking to.

Avoid slogans. Many people include their company slogan in their introduction, "I'm Julie Smith with A-1 Office Supply. *We put the clip on your paper!*" While this approach may seem snappy and clever, it actually makes you appear disingenuous. Slogans are very effective marketing tools, but they must be employed at the right time and place. Let's discuss where and when they can be used.

There are two kinds of marketing: *One-to-One Marketing*, and *One-to-Many Marketing*. One-to-Many Marketing is one piece of advertising that reaches many people at once; websites, social media, billboards, TV commercials, brochures, and business cards. One-to-Many Marketing is where slogans do their best work. If the slogan is clever, funny, relatable, or thought-provoking, it can engage the viewer and spark interest. However, networking is a face-to-face, One-to-One Marketing environment, where slogans have the opposite effect. Face-to-face, slogans don't spark interest, they sound phony. While networking, stick to real conversation; leave the slogans for your website.

Be an I, not a we. There is a tendency for people who represent a large organization to say "we do this" instead of "I do this." They say, "At XYZ Company, we specialize in…" There is nothing inherently wrong with presenting yourself as part of a larger organization, but remember, we are interested in working with you because *you* are the one we are meeting. It is comforting for the prospect to know that the person they will get when they call or e-mail is the same person with whom they are sharing conversation and appetizers.

When people choose to work with you, they aren't really buying your company, they are buying you. Speak in terms of what *you* do, not your company. If their needs are best met by someone else at your company, let them know that you have the perfect person for them to meet, but that *you* will introduce them and be there to make sure the relationship is a good one. Networking is a lot like dating. Imagine meeting someone at a party who was charming and attractive, only to have them say, "It's been great getting to know you. Now I am going to pass you off to someone else." Wouldn't you feel cheated?

Lighten up! When I ask people what makes other people's introductions so memorable, most often it is because "They were funny!"

> Adage from the *National Speakers Association*
> "Does my speech have to include humor?"
> "Only if you want to get paid."

The power that laughter holds in commanding people's attention and influencing their behavior is immeasurable. Laughter cements a relationship, seals a deal, and positions a leader. Here is why:

Laughter makes you memorable. As I mentioned earlier, one of the greatest challenges of networking is to be the one person the prospect remembers out of all the people they encounter. Typically, if we want someone to remember us, we add weight to our message. This does follow the rule that memory calls for urgency, but too much urgency causes stress, and too much stress either destroys memory or distorts it. When you laugh, however, the subject of the laughter is instantly transferred to long-term memory. Happy memories are more easily recalled.

Laughter creates agreement. At its core, laughter is a social form of agreement. The reason we laugh at stories, jokes, and satirical statements is that we agree with the message they carry. We consider people with whom we share laugh to be agreeable folks, and we want to be around them more.

Laughter eases tension. Networking functions or chance encounters always carry a bit of tension. No-one is sure how the interaction will go. Releasing this tension by sparking laughter makes you everyone's hero.

Laughter makes you socially smart. Research about laughter in social settings (as opposed to sitting alone watching a funny movie) revealed a surprising finding; people who laugh are more socially intelligent even if they didn't create the laughter. It is easy to see why the *laugh producer* would have to be socially adept in order to elicit laughter from others. However, even those who simply laugh along with the group have been shown to be more socially intelligent than those who sit silently while those around them laugh.

The reason laughter increases your social IQ is that laughing along with a group requires the ability to accurately interpret dozens of subtle cues from the people around you. To know just when to laugh, how much, and how long takes quite a bit of brain work. The more you laugh along with people, the more you hone the ability to read people in all situations, humorous or otherwise.

Laughter gives you social power. It is an little known fact that the first person to make a group of people laugh has the most social power in that group. Inspiring laughter in others demonstrates social confidence. Everyone knows that attempting humor in a group of people, especially a group that has yet to laugh together, carries a big risk. What if no-one laughs? People understand the risk involved with trying to be funny in front of strangers, so the mere attempt at humor shows that you are willing to take social risks; an important sign of confidence.

Remember, it doesn't matter if your attempt at humor falls a little flat, as long as you show that this minor stumble doesn't bother you. If you can shrug off a small misstep in a social setting, we know you won't crumble when the stakes are higher.

Laughter makes you more hire-able. Add all these benefits up and you become a person who is memorable, likeable, powerful, and confident. Who wouldn't want to hire someone with all those qualities?

I'm not suggesting that you become the comedian of the group. We have all met a jokester who doesn't know when to stop being funny. Humor is about balancing the funny and the serious. And creating laughter isn't about telling jokes, it is about being yourself and sharing your story. That opens the door to laughter. If you want to learn more about humor, there is a great book, *What We Laugh At...and Why*, written by a genius on the subject, Stevie Ray.

If you want to tell people the truth,
you'd better make them laugh or they'll kill you.
George Bernard Shaw

CHAPTER 5

Get Out of the Prom Circle

The *Prom Circle* is that group of people you always see at networking functions. Just like at a high school dance, people gather only with people they know, huddled tightly in a circle to make sure no strangers can invade; leaving the safety of the circle only when their drinks are empty. This makes for great socializing, but terrible networking. And no one has yet to create the means to network that doesn't involve meeting strangers.

Some organizations are so frustrated with the Prom Circle phenomenon that they create games that force people to mingle. They ring a bell every fifteen minutes so that people must leave the group they are in and talk to someone new. Or, like a networking version of speed dating, everyone sits in a big circle facing each other. When the buzzer sounds, the inner circle rotates while the outer circle waits for their new match; hoping for a love connection. At one event I attended, the rule also included having to exchange business cards before you switched partners. The organizer's hearts were in the right place, but, since the session was so regimented, little interest was actually generated that would foster wanting the business card of each *date*. The other problem with structured networking is that you lose the ability to develop two crucial skills needed to network; getting out of conversations gracefully, and entering existing conversations smoothly.

To combat the urge to socialize only with familiar faces, and to build the skills of *getting in and getting out*, I teach a game during my workshops aptly named, *Prom Circle*. This is a good game to play with colleagues. A roomful of people stand in groups of two, three, or four people. They begin conversations about whatever topics they wish. While they are talking, I circulate throughout the room and tap various people the shoulder (choosing only one person from each group). Whoever is tapped must leave their group and find a new group to join. The goal is to leave a conversation gracefully and enter another conversation smoothly. If you think that this is easy, it isn't. And I have hundreds of uncomfortable workshop participants to prove it. Before starting the exercise, remind the participants that, even though everyone knows the *tap, you leave* rule, they shouldn't just walk away as soon as they are tapped. They should act as if the situation were an actual networking event. Unless, of course, you actually do just walk away from people on the spur of the moment. If so, this book can't help you.

When circulating the room, I select people to tap on the shoulder based on the situation they are in. Some people are leading the conversation in their group; I tap them because it is good practice to learn to exit a group even though you are the center of attention. Sometimes you find yourself the leader of a conversation, but you realize that none of the people in the group are good prospects. You can't say to yourself, "There is no business to be gained here, but I can't leave because I'm the hub of the conversation." When you determine that is it time to network with better prospects, it is time to leave the group.

I tap other people because they are the opposite of the hub. The conversation is going on around them, but they aren't a part of it. These people need to exit as well. It may seem easier because the attention is not on them, but they still need to exit without simply walking away. Finally, some people are in pairs and I want to see how they can gracefully end a conversation when it is just the two of them. This is probably the most difficult exit to make without seeming abrupt or rude. On the surface, this game seems simple; just say goodbye to your group and find another person or group to join. You would be amazed at how difficult it can be, and how clumsy some people are at performing this type of social etiquette.

I let the *Prom Circle* exercise go on for about fifteen minutes, or enough time for me to tap every participant at least once. At the end of the exercise I ask for feedback. For those who were tapped, what did it feel like to leave a group mid-conversation? For the people who had someone leave their group, did the person exit well? How well did people enter an existing conversation? Even the smallest action has a profound impact on the impression left on others. First, for those who had to exit their group, some politely acknowledged everyone before leaving, while others just turned and walked away. No goodbyes. No "It was nice to meet you." Just gone. I imagine these people at home getting ready to leave for a long business trip. Their children are lined up at the door to say goodbye and he dashes out the back door. "Where did daddy go? He was here a minute ago!"

When I ask workshop participants how it felt if someone abruptly left the group, they say "Kinda bad. We wondered what happened. Was it something we said?" Isn't it funny that, even though the participants are fully aware that it is a networking exercise, and not the real thing, they still feel jilted because they didn't receive a proper good-bye? Networking is about building relationships, and all relationships, no matter how brief, need the same things; a *getting to know you* period, a foundation of common interest, and a sense of fun and laughter. But the most important element of a relationship is a sense of closure; a feeling of being acknowledged. Knowing that the effort we put forth on behalf of our partner is respected.

Psychologists will tell you that one of the most difficult sources of anguish for people is when a relationship ends without a sense of closure. Even a conversation of a few minutes demands some kind of closure before you move on. Acknowledge the other people by telling them it was good to meet them. Respect them by finding an appropriate time to exit. And provide closure by telling them you hope to meet up with them again soon.

Don't lie! For some reason, some people feel the need to make up an excuse to leave their group, "I have to take a phone call" or "I told my babysitter I would call at 9:00" or "The president wants me to fly to Washington to discuss his foreign policy bill." I was discussing the need to make a graceful exit at a corporate workshop and a man raised his hand and said "I have the perfect way to get out of any conversation. I just tell people that I have to go to the men's room." And he was serious. After the room stopped chuckling, I told him that there are two problems with this strategy. One is that people will notice that he leaves the group without actually going to the restroom. Or he does indeed go to the restroom every time he leaves a group, and people start to wonder what is wrong with his bladder.

The bigger problem with this, and any other strategy, is that people can tell if you are lying. There is never the need to lie to move to another conversation. This is networking, not dating. People know that the purpose of the event is to meet new prospects and gain business. Simply tell the truth, "It was really great to meet you. I want to make sure that I meet as many people as I can tonight, so I'm going to excuse myself. Hopefully we'll reconnect again before the night is over." You have acknowledged them, and provided closure.

Be memorable. You can network all you want, but if people don't remember you, it was all a waste of time. When you leave a group, try to make a lasting impression. Remember from earlier in the book, whatever people laugh about transfers to long-term memory. When you leave a group, leave them with something fun. You don't have to have a joke for every occasion, just keep your eyes and ears open for something you can comment on that will produce a chuckle. The next day, few people will remember exactly what was discussed during the evenings conversations, but they will remember who made them laugh.

If you are concerned about using appropriate humor (and you should be), humor pointed at yourself is always safe. While I was networking during a business function one evening, I realized it was time to move on to meet more people. I said to my group, "Oh no, the caterer just walked in. I'm really a busboy and I'm not supposed to be talking to the guests. Gotta go!" After people laughed, I provided actual closure by telling them I was off to meet some other people, and that it was great to talk to them.

Humor pointed at someone else in the group can be a bit riskier, but it is fairly easy to tell who in the group loves being the center of attention. Those who love the limelight will love you for putting them in it. "Well folks, I promised Bob I would keep his groupies away from him for the night and I see that a bunch of autograph seekers got past security again. I'll be back later." I always back up a funny statement with a sincere note of closure.

To add a bit more respect and memorable-ness to my exit, I often refer to something specific in the conversation. "Jennifer, I would be interested in talking with you more about your new project. I have a couple of ideas that you might be able to use. Why don't I call you tomorrow to schedule a meeting to talk them over?" Focusing on the needs of others during the conversation provides great closure and makes for a more memorable you.

Leaving a Prom Circle is only half the battle. There is also the task of entering another group smoothly. I wish you could be a fly on the wall at some of my workshops. Invariably, I will tap someone on the shoulder, they say their goodbyes and make a graceful exit, then freeze in the middle of the room. Their eyes move from group to group, unable to decide which one to join or, when they do find a suitable group, they are unable to figure out how to smoothly enter. It is like watching a high school kid standing in the middle of the cafeteria at lunch time, holding a tray of food and scanning the room looking for one face he recognizes.

Entering an existing conversation doesn't have to be a big deal, but adults seem to make it so. Watch a six-year old child dropped off at a day-care center. She will run up to the first child she sees and say, "I'm Wendy, what's your name? Do you want to play?" Within seconds, the two children are playing and having a great time. Adults, on the other hand, will wander aimlessly until we see some small opening, then we'll creep into the group as if we hope no one will notice us.

At one workshop, I tapped a woman on the shoulder and she gave me the most pained expression. She said, "Oh no. Now I've got to meet different people!" She left her circle and stood in the middle of the room looking from group to group. She never joined another group. She stood nervously by herself until I stopped the exercise. When I asked her why she didn't join another group she explained that if she saw a group of people fully engaged in conversation, she felt like she would be intruding. Furthermore, she pointed at one group that was laughing uproariously and said that she would feel even more like an outsider because they were having such fun. The group she was referring to—the big laughing group—replied, "Are you kidding? We were having such a great time we would have welcomed you to join us!"

See how much adults can overthink a situation? And before you criticize this woman too harshly, think back to the last event you attended. Didn't you have moments when you thought, "I don't want to join that group, I don't know anyone there. And I don't want to join that other group, they're all dressed fancier than me. Those people over there look too buddy-buddy for me to join." I learned a valuable lesson in networking from, of all people, my step-daughter, Ondine. When Ondine was eleven years old, my wife, Kanitta, took her to the park to play one evening. I was on my way home and got a call. Kanitta said, "Instead of going home, come to the park. We're here playing." When I arrived, I saw Ondine playing with another eleven-year-old girl. Kanitta said, "Ondine saw her on the swings, walked up and said, 'Hi. I'm Ondine. Want to be friends?' The other girl thought for a moment and said, 'Sure. My name is Ava.' They have been playing ever since."

I looked around the park and saw another couple on a park bench on the other side of the playground. By the way they were watching the girls play, they were obviously Ava's parents. Being the mature adults that we were, Kanitta and I sat on our park bench while the other couple sat on theirs. Eventually Ondine and Ava walked up to us and demanded, "Why aren't you making friends with them?" Kanitta and I stammered out some weak response, to which they replied, "Go over there and make friends!" We sheepishly walked over to the other couple and said, "Our daughter said we had to be friends with you." Our families have been friends ever since.

Being social animals, humans instinctively dissect social situations so we can determine how to best manage them. We certainly shouldn't be like six-year olds, running brazenly up to everyone and screaming, "Let's play!" However, we could take a lesson from children and dial down the analyzing enough to remove the fears that ruin networking.

The goal of networking is to make those around you feel comfortable. If your timidity requires others to work harder on your behalf, you are not a welcome sight. If you don't provide a smooth closure to the conversation, your partner will feel uncomfortable. And, if you overcompensate for feeling nervous by barging into conversations, you cause stress. If you enter the group weakly, the rest will have to do more work by taking on the role of host, welcoming you in and introducing you to the group. Those who cause more work are seen as a burden. We don't want to do business with burdens. The next time you are at a networking function, give yourself a mental tap on the shoulder every now and then. This will keep you from staying with the same comfortable group the entire time. The next time you are at a conference and the group breaks for lunch, try sitting with a table of people you've never met. Practicing the vital skill of meeting new people in non-threatening environments will make you much smoother when moment-of-truth networking opportunities arise.

CHAPTER 6

Now What Do I Say?

Networking can be intimidating because there is so much added pressure on the conversation. Familial relationships are great because you can trip over your words or misspeak without fear of everyone running out of the room or laughing in your face (unless you are in my family). In networking, there is the pressure of never knowing if we are going to say something supremely stupid. This pressure is not entirely unwarranted. With the myriad cultures and norms around, it isn't easy to know what is conversationally out of bounds.

A case in point, I was at an event with an international audience when one man said to his dinner table guests, "I've been sitting on my fanny for a while, so I'm going to stretch my legs before the program begins." Three British women at the table looked aghast. What the man didn't know was that, in British countries, *fanny* is a slang term for female genitalia. He also learned that there are some things you just can't unsay. Fortunately, the British women were understanding, but it is a safe bet that, whenever they saw the man after that, there was a tinge of discomfort. I have personally racked up my share of faux pas, as well. During a trip to Japan, I was explaining some of the games we play with little children and got around to the classic, *Got Your Nose* game. This is the game where you pinch the nose of a little child between your first and second fingers, pull gently, then quickly poke the tip of your thumb through your fingers to make it look like you pulled off the tip of their nose; saying, "I got your nose." My Japanese friends didn't seem at all amused by the game, and quickly made their exits to talk to others. At that point, my Japanese host said, "Stevie. In Japan, that gesture is the same as giving the finger." So, I essentially told my Japanese hosts that Americans take great delight in flipping off our children.

Cultural fumbles aside, we can tend to place so much importance on everything we say that our words never measure up to our expectations. While driving home after an event we think back and over-analyze every conversation, thinking "Why did I say that?!" Good networking, however, isn't about saying just the right thing, it is about saying what you want in the right way. The first step is to realize an important fact about conversation; nobody is listening to you. There now, doesn't that make you feel better?

If the most important goal of networking is to make a good connection with a prospect and to have that person like you, your conversation must engage the other person's *Approach Response*. To do that, you have to understand how the brain operates. And it doesn't work quite the way people think. Most of us think that, during conversation, the brain analyzes what is said and stores the information so we can access it later. Not true. This is because of what we spoke of earlier in the book, that the least efficient function of the human brain is information processing. Think back to the last presentation you attended. If there was a lot of detailed information being presented, your mind shut down only a few minutes into the lecture. You started noticing odd little things in the room—what people next to you were doing, quirky mannerisms about the speaker—anything to avoid mentally trudging through the information being presented. You soon find yourself thinking, "I don't have to pay attention; this will be in the handout."

You can see why most networking conversations fall flat while social conversations don't. Social conversations are less data-driven. There is no expected outcome to the conversation, just pleasant talk, so the brain is less taxed. However, networking conversations can often contain too much information. People are so eager to tell you about their business that they load you up with detail; and detail stresses the brain. In the end, while someone drones on and on, we just nod and smile, but we're thinking, "Just kill me now!"

I was at a networking function and struck up a conversation with a man who worked for a computer software company. The conversation started out fine because he had asked about another association that I worked for. The association I spoke of was experiencing problems with their website and he was giving me some possible solutions. I was interested because he did a great job of connecting his information to my needs. Then things went south. He wanted me to know about his company, so he started describing an incredibly complicated web-based document service he developed. Anyone looking at my face could tell I was utterly confused about this technology. Anyone, that is, but this guy. He describing every facet of the service in great detail. I went from really liking this guy and planning to refer business to him, to being so confused that I tossed his business card in the trash when I got back to my office. I wasn't going to risk referring this guy to my trusted colleagues.

Remember also that the brain's most efficient function is pattern recognition. The brain instantly discerns patterns in the world around us so that we may develop habits; which lead to productivity as well as safety. Our connection to someone else is formed at the most basic neurological level; the level of emotions. Because emotions are a product of patterned behavior in the brain, not cognitive analysis, we don't determine whether we like someone on an intellectual level and then develop emotional ties with that person. Quite the opposite. We develop an emotional connection and then justify that connection intellectually.

This is why some of the most common advice about networking is not accurate. For instance, people are often told that an important networking skill is to remember people's names and faces; that remembering someone's name will flatter them and develop a better connection. This is not entirely false, but someone remembering our name is not sufficient to make us truly trust and connect with them. On its own, remembering names and faces is a mental parlor trick. It might be flattering to hear your own name, or to feel important enough to be remembered, but I have had many occasions where someone remembered my name and I still found him or her distasteful. Conversely, I have had people admit, "I'm sorry, I forgot your name," but they were so genuine and likeable that the misstep didn't matter in the least. Parlor tricks don't lead to positive emotional connections.

If, by this point in the chapter, you are thinking, "But Stevie hasn't answered the question of 'What do I say?'" you are right. The internet is filled with websites that claim to have the perfect conversation starters, and (pardon my boldness), they're all crap. Any prepared line to get a conversation going, or keep it rolling, is no different than an *Elevator Pitch*. I have been the victim of people who, I was positive, had a line at the ready just in case the conversation needed a boost. No one likes talking to those people.

CHAPTER 7

Common Questions

This being the second edition of the book, I have had several questions posed by clients that could be of some use to you while sharpening your networking skills. I could have incorporated these tidbits into the chapter on *Do This, Don't Do That*, but then it wouldn't seem like I did a bunch of extra work for the second edition, would it? One additional thought, when you read some of the questions I have been asked, you might think "That is ridiculously simple," and skip to the next one. I often found myself thinking the same thing. However, I discovered that, because a question was posed about an issue I had previously dismissed as common knowledge, I was forced to revisit how I approach the situation. It turned out to be a good exercise in self-examination and self-improvement. I encourage you to approach the following questions in the same manner.

Shake it baby!

I conducted a networking workshop that had an interesting audience. Part of the group was a local chapter of marketing professionals, and another group were public relations professionals. They also invited students from a local university business college, and business students from two high schools. So the room was filled with everyone from the nearly retired to the not-yet-looking-for-work. It was fun to see the varying styles of interaction and conversation, given there were four generations in the same workshop.

At one point, a high school student raised her hand and admitted, "I have never been taught how to give a proper handshake." The expressions around the room revealed that, while the older adults considered the skill a basic part of business training, they forgot that kids aren't being raised with quite as much attention to etiquette as in *the olden days*. It was certainly a fair question, given how many of us have suffered through bad handshakes. You either get some bruiser trying to prove his manhood by crushing the metacarpals and phalanges in your right hand. Or you get the *fish grip*; a handshake so lacking in pressure you wonder how the person is able to open a peanut butter jar at home.

And handshakes are as different from country to country as clothing and food; if a handshake is performed in that country at all. Given that, if you plan to travel, you will likely search for proper business etiquette in your destination country, we will stick to the good ol' U.S. of A. grip and grin. The type of handshake a particular culture embraces is a product of, among other things, standard distance for personal space in that culture. The closer the space, the more physical contact is allowed for the handshake.

The most common personal space distance in America is about three feet, which allows for our one-hand-to-one-hand handshake. The crook of your thumb rests in the crook of the other person's thumb, and the grip is firm without being hard.

After explaining this, the young woman at the workshop asked, "How long do you hang on?" The room laughed, meaning that more than one person had been victim to *the person who wouldn't let go!* The standard in America is two-three shakes of the hand, then release. But the best advice for how hard, and how long, to grip, is to take your cue from your partner. Match their pressure, and when they release, you release. If they try to let go and you don't, you're the creepy one.

Many cultures do not practice physical touching at all. Muslims must pray five times each day, and they must maintain *ablution*, or physical cleanliness, for each prayer. Since the hands are one part of the body a Muslim must keep clean for prayer, it is easier to avoid physical contact than it is to continually wash throughout the day. And religious tradition prevents men and women from shaking hands at all, unless that particular individual prefers it. Latin American countries allow for much more physical contact, so their handshakes could involve two hands; one either covering the top of the handshake, or gripping the elbow of the receiver. In America, such a handshake is considered more personal and informal. When in doubt as to the appropriate greeting, watch your partner for cues.

Just tell me what you want

At one workshop, a woman asked, "When is it okay to come right out and state what you want? To make *the ask*?" Asking for business can certainly be a delicate balance between too soon (thus appearing self-serving and desperate) or too late (appearing vague and unfocused). Earlier in the book, I equated networking to dating. If you see a prospective romantic interest at a party, you don't just walk up and say, "Will you marry me?" At least, not if you would like to avoid restraining orders. On the other hand, if you spend too much time with idle chit-chat, without making your interest known, the other person is left wondering about your intentions.

People like to know where they stand, and they like to know what you want, but the fear of rejection can cause us to dance around the subject, thereby missing opportunities. My answer to the woman at the workshop was, first establish common ground. See if there is something you can do for each other so the relationship isn't parasitic. Then, instead of talking about your ultimate goal, state exactly what you want the other person to do. Saying, "I am trying to expand my client base," puts the other person in a tough spot. Few people can wave their magic wand and have customers flock to your door. Also, "more clients" is too vague. It doesn't tell the other person what they can do to help you.

However, if you say, "I am trying to expand my list of clients who are small businesses with about 20-30 employees who could use help lowering their health insurance costs. Would you be able to recommend four possible clients you know who fit this category?" everyone knows if they can offer recommendations. They either know clients who fit the category or not. And asking for a specific number (four possible clients) and a specific action (recommend them to you) lets the other person know exactly what they need to do to help you. The more specific *the ask*, the greater your chances for success. Use asks like "Can I call you to get this information? When would be a good day and time?" "If I send this information, can you forward it to X number of people?" The clearer you are about your *ask*, the more professional you appear, and the easier it is to work with you. Others will see that this is how you do business, and believe that doing business with you more in the future will promise the same clarity and focus.

It's not you, it's me

Along the lines of when to make *the ask*, is when to say goodbye to a prospect. A man stopped me after a workshop and said that he routinely met prospects over lunch or coffee several times. The problem is he was sometimes unsure as to whether the meetings would ultimately lead to business. Besides needing to take a note from the previous section about making *the ask*, he needs to go one step further and clarify the relationship. Lunch and coffee are great, but if you aren't getting business out of it, you had better be happy shifting the relationship into the category labeled, *Social*.

Personally, I have never been insulted by honesty (unless it was my step-daughter giving her honest opinion about my jokes). There is nothing wrong with, at the outset of networking, letting your partner know that you will ultimately be seeking a mutually beneficial business relationship. It is still fine to chat about family, hobbies, and the like as the relationship develops, but both parties know that if business doesn't eventually grow, the relationship might end.

Humans hate endings; especially when we have invested time and effort in the relationship. Neurologists have discovered that our brains are actually wired this way. We have an *in for a penny, in for a pound* mentality. This is why people who lose $5,000 while gambling will rarely say to themselves, "I've lost enough. I should quit." Instead, they think, "I have to keep betting in order to win back what I lost." History is filled with people doubling down on their actions simply because they already took three steps toward a goal and their brains said, "You've already gone this far, keep going!"

The best way to judge whether it is time to pull the plug is to first be conscious of whether you are truly building a lasting, mutually beneficial relationship, or just taking the fourth step because you already took the first three. It is a good idea to include the other person in the conversation. And honesty is best. "I have really enjoyed our meetings, and I want to respect the goal we agreed to, which is to help each other's business. Since we haven't reached that point yet, I wanted to get your perspective. Do you still think we have something to offer each other? If not, we can move on in other directions and keep in each other in mind for future projects." You can always bet that, if you are wondering whether a business relationship is mutually beneficial, so is the other person.

Referrals

Many people have heard of the *80/20 Rule*, the theory that 80% of a company's sales will come from 20% of its clients, but I would bet that most don't know that the rule is based on gardening. In 1896, an Italian economist Vilfredo Pareto, published a paper while at the University of Lausanne, which noted that 80% of effects (of all kinds), come from 20% of the causes of those effects. He first noticed this while in his garden, where he saw that 80% of peas came from 20% of the pods. Joseph Juran, a management consultant born in 1904, connected Pareto's theory to business and sales, dubbing it the *Pareto Principle*.

The Pareto Principle is a good reminder for us to focus our energies more on building business using our highest performing existing clients, rather than constantly chasing new customers. Of course, this rule must be adjusted depending on your *sales cycle*. The sales cycle refers to the series of predictable phases required to sell a product or service. Depending on your product, these phases usually include, Prospecting, Initial Contact, Identify Needs, Present the Offer, Manage Objections, Close the Sale, and Repeat Sales/Referrals.

The rule of thumb is, the longer the sales cycle for your product, the more clients you need in the *pipeline*. The pipeline refers to the number of clients you must consistently engage with in order to keep sales flowing. Products with a longer sales cycle, such as automobiles or houses, demand a big pipeline that is constantly being filled. IHS Automotive reports that the average American buys 9.4 cars during his or her lifetime. Compare that to candy, where one in four Americans will have a piece of candy every day of the week. Automobile dealers can't rely on 20% of their customers to keep them afloat, but Hershey's knows that they have a loyal following of choco-holics.

The last phase of the sales cycle is Repeat Sales/Referrals. It feels great to do such good work that our clients actually go out of their way to get others to buy from us, but, as they say, *Hope is not a strategy*. You can't simply do good work and hope that people will spread the word. My company learned this the hard way. Since opening in 1989, the corporate training division of our business grew steadily year after year. Because there aren't many ways to advertise corporate training services, we relied on word of mouth and promotional activities, but mostly word of mouth. After being in business long enough, whenever we asked a new client "How did you hear about us?" they usually said "One of our committee members saw you at a convention." We mistakenly assumed that, as long as we wowed the audience, the phone would keep ringing (or, in later years, our e-mail inbox would stay filled).

Then the year 2008 happened. If you were living on a small island during that time with no access to the outside world, 2008 began the Great Recession; or, in economic jargon, *a really crappy time*. Our company actually did quite well during the beginning of the recession. For the first number of years, we still grew sales, so we thought that we were somehow immune to its devastation; that our service was just so darned good that losing money was for other people. After all, we had experienced twenty straight years of growth. Nothing to worry about!

Suddenly, 2015 ended with half the revenue than 2014. What happened? We didn't keep the pipeline full. We relied on chance to direct our referrals. While other companies attacked the recession with bold new strategies and increased focus on sales, we played a game called *Business as Usual*. We had forgotten the advice of more experienced colleagues, "If you don't keep the pipeline full, your upward rollercoaster ride will eventually head downward." Keeping your pipeline full is a step toward evening out the rollercoaster and keeping sales steady. Ever since then, we balance our activities between serving current clients as well as building new relationships; and a big part of that is getting referrals.

To do this, we took a lesson from Marshall, the member of our board of directors I mentioned earlier in the book. If you recall, Marshall is one of those salesmen who always wins the *Sales of the Year Award*, no matter what he sells or who he is selling for. Naturally, other sales professionals want to know his secrets. One question that he is always asked is, "How do you get so many referrals?" Marshall tells them that he has a secret weapon for getting clients to refer him to new prospects. He says, "I ask." Younger sales people always look shocked at the boldness of this strategy, but Marshall says, "If I do a good job for someone, I have no problem saying, 'I would really like to work with other companies like yours. If what I did was beneficial to you, can you tell me the names of some other people, and would you mind letting them know I am going to call so they know that you endorse me?" He reminds other sales professionals, "I never ask for referrals unless I know I did a good job for the client. And I never ask for referrals by text or e-mail. Don't be a wuss, get on the phone. If you did a good job for someone, they like to repay your hard work by helping you out."

I have used this simple philosophy whenever I host performances at *Stevie Ray's Comedy Cabaret*. The cabaret represents the entertainment side of our business, where we perform comedy improv shows each weekend, year round. Being busy with corporate workshops, I rarely get the chance to host shows at my cabaret anymore, but when I do I get to connect with the audience in a way that actors in a traditional play cannot. With improv, you don't simply perform a show and leave, you actually talk to the audience and build a connection.

Like any other business, entertainment venues rely heavily on word of mouth. Advertising is cost prohibitive, and there are so many other options for entertainment—movies, concerts, nightclubs, theatre, or staying at home and watching Netflix—that we need the audience to talk us up to friends in order to remain competitive. In short, we need to ask for referrals, and make sure *the ask* will result in more clients.

I'm sure you have been to a show where, after the final bow, the director says, "If you enjoyed tonight's performance, please tell a friend." Whenever I hear that plea, it goes in one ear and out the other. I never actually feel the urge to refer a friend because *the ask* doesn't feel genuine. Referrals are given on behalf of a friend or trusted colleague. Only part of the urge to refer a product or service is so our friends can experience something great ("Hey, all you Facebook friends. If you are looking for a great night of comedy, you have to go to Stevie Ray's Comedy Cabaret!"). The other reason to refer is so we can help someone we like grow their business. Quite often, if I have been served well by a company, I refer them to others because I want to see that nice company be rewarded for their efforts.

So, at the end of the show at my cabaret, I don't rush through a standard *tell your friends* speech. I make it personal, and specific. I say, "We loved having all of you here tonight, and we would love to have more people just like you. So, can you do me a favor? Before you go to bed tonight, or when you get up tomorrow morning, post on Facebook, write an e-mail, or send a Tweet that says 'I had a great time at Stevie Ray's Comedy Cabaret. The comedy was clean and the show was hilarious.' Can you do that for me?"

If you dissect my *ask*, you will see it is crafted to elicit a specific outcome. *Do me a favor*, gets the audience thinking about who they are helping. Not just a nameless, faceless, company, but a person they like. *Before you go to bed*, gives a timeline. Without a deadline, the brain stores the request in the *I'll get to that someday* file. *Post on Facebook, write an e-mail*, tells the audience exactly what I want them to do. If you aren't specific, the other person doesn't know what to do. And they will not take the energy to figure it out on their own; that's not their job. *I had a great time at*, tells them what I want them to say about me. At Stevie Ray's Improv Company, we know what our brand is, and we want the audience to promote that brand. If you leave it up to the other person to decide what to say about you, you have no control over the message. I want others to know we offer clean comedy that is slap-your-knee funny, so that is what I tell people to say. And frankly, people like it when you tell them what to say about you. It makes the job of referring less work. Finally, *Can you do that for me?* cements the agreement. Once people agree to an action, they are committed. In the case of *Stevie Ray's Comedy Cabaret*, the audience applauds to signal their agreement to refer us to friends. In the case of networking, the agreement is sealed with a *Yes, I can do that for you*, and a handshake.

If you would just stop talking, I could listen better

A workshop participant asked, "When is it okay to interrupt when someone is talking? I try to listen intently, but sometimes they mention something that I would really like to know more about, but the only way to ask is to interrupt them." The reason I appreciated her question so much is that so many people carelessly interrupt others without knowing the damage it does to the relationship.

Networking is not just about meeting new prospects and determining if a mutually beneficial relationship is possible. It is a delicate dance. It is our opportunity to size up a person as *safe/not safe, honest/dishonest*, or *trustworthy/unreliable*. When you speak, the listener is only half-listening to your words. They are also paying attention to how well you read signals and respond accordingly. When someone is on a roll and you break their concentration, you demonstrate much more than the inability to adjust to others' communication needs, you exhibit unprofessional behavior.

Of course, not all instances of speaking during another person's speaking is harmful to the conversation. It is here when we make the distinction between an *interruption* and an *interjection*. Quite simply, an interruption is breaking the flow of the speaker's thought or direction; whereas an interjection is voicing a quick addition to the conversation. Interjections accomplish positive outcomes; they:

1) Voice agreement, "You're right" or "Yes, I've seen that, too."
2) Keep the conversation moving in the direction the speaker intended, "How does that work?" or "What happened next?"
3) Validate your partner's intent.
4) Demonstrate attentiveness, "Uh huh" "I see" or "I didn't know that."

Condition #1, voicing agreement, is not to suggest that you must agree with whatever your partner says. To do so would display disingenuousness. However, you must disagree the right way. If you allow the other person their point of view, while still maintaining yours, you display a mature sense of the nature of relationships. If, however, the other person must be *wrong* in order for you to be *right*, don't expect your phone to ring with new business. I have a good friend, Dave, who is easily one of the most well-read individuals on Earth. If you bring up a topic of conversation, chances are good that Dave has read an article about it. And it won't be a short essay in *People Magazine*, Dave will have read a peer-reviewed publication in a report that is only granted to members of Mensa. The nice thing about having a conversation with Dave is that if you say something inaccurate, he can correct your information without making you feel wrong. Instead of, "That's not right, because I read that..." he will say (in a gentle, non-threatening tone), "I've heard that, too, but there is some really great research now that suggests something different. I think, since you are interested in this subject, you would find it fascinating." He actually turns a correction into a compliment.

Condition #3 is important because good relationships depend on people feeling like the other person *gets* them. If someone tells a story, and the intent is to get a laugh at the end, and you don't laugh, not only are you not validating the intent of the story, you aren't validating the person telling the story. You don't *get* them. The discomfort caused by this schism will result in the speaker distancing from you, and avoiding further contact.

I have experienced this schism many times—the feeling that I didn't want to talk to my networking partner any longer—and it was only after examining the conversation deeper that I realized that the reason for my discomfort was the lack of support from my partner for the intent of my story. In one instance, I was talking to an engineer at a corporate function. We were talking about the design of a particular automobile when I mentioned that I thought a certain change the manufacturer made didn't make sense to me. The engineer said, "It makes perfect sense to me." Now, since the engineer has more experience with design than I do, he could be right, and the design change could make perfect sense. I still left the conversation feeling like a fool. I thought, "I bet my friend Dave could have enlightened me about the design without making me feel wrong for my initial opinion." I quickly left the conversation with the engineer and avoided him for the rest of the evening.

Another instance was at an IT convention, (since it involved IT, you can probably guess where this is going). When I related a story to an IT specialist about my trying to solve a computer issue in my office, and that I was confused right from the start of the process, my intent was to acknowledge how difficult his profession was, and to lighten up our conversation. He immediately launched into all the steps I needed to take to solve my computer problem. An interjection would have been appropriate on his part had I asked, "What do you think I should have done?" But I didn't. Since I only offered as much information in my story to keep the topic surface-level, his interjection would have been better received had he said, "You are so right. Computers can drive us all crazy. Hey, let me know the next time you get in the weeds. I love helping people with computer problems and taking away the stress." Believe me, had he said that, I would have asked for his business card.

To demonstrate command of conversation, and of people, it is important to ask yourself "What is the intent of this person's story?" If it is to surprise you with a quirky ending, show surprise. If it is to elicit laughter, laugh. If it is to express frustration, share their irritation. The ability to show empathy is considered an advanced skill among humans. It goes along with the advice I gave a student of mine many years ago. She was one of those people who would let you get about half-way into your story before interrupting and talking about her own experience with your situation. Except, of course, that her experience was much more interesting. I sat her down during an evaluation meeting once and said, "You need to be as interested in other people's stories as you are in your own."

A discussion about interruptions versus interjections certainly wouldn't be complete without discussing the difference between men and women when it comes to cutting into the conversation. It is no secret that men interrupt more than women. Especially not if you are a woman who has ever tried to finish telling a man a story. Adrienne Hancock, a linguist at George Washington University, conducted a study in 2014 that tracked short conversations between same gender and mixed gender partners. She discovered that, when men were speaking with women, they interrupted an average of 2.1 instances over a three-minute conversation. Interruptions dropped to 1.8 instances for male-to-male conversations. In another study, Kieran Snyder, a Ph.D. in linguistics from the University of Pennsylvania, tracked conversations in business environments—staff meetings, conferences—and discovered that men will interrupt women once every two minutes, fifty one seconds. The study determined that, not only did men interrupt twice as often as women, but they interrupted women three times as often as they interrupted other men.

There are many theories as to why men interrupt more. The most common being that men more often view interactions with a competitive eye. Some psychologists link the process of conversation to early man's mating rituals.

The male that demonstrated dominance in the tribe was rewarded with the best mate. As humans evolved (well, most of us) we replaced physical battles with verbal jousting. Quite simply, the quiet man is seen as the weak man. This is only a theory, and many psychologists disagree; citing simple socialization as the culprit. Some neurologists point to the fact that the wiring in the female brain for communication is spread throughout the entire cranial system, whereas men's communication wiring is located in a central core. They believe this gives men and women different communication processes that affect listening, processing, and response. Some psychologists believe that it is inaccurate to assume that, when one person is speaking and another interrupts the conversation, that the initial speaker is a victim in the first place.

Theories aside, blindly interrupting and redirecting a conversation without being mindful of you partner is a dangerous habit. Remember earlier in the book when I suggested that conversation is like two children playing catch with a ball? The most important goal in *catch* is that the ball doesn't hit the ground. If it does, you have to wait for the other kid to retrieve the ball, which is a pain! The game of catch only works when the person throwing the ball knows the person catching is ready to receive. It is a game of perfect cooperation, because you only get the ball when it is your turn, and you give it away when it is your partner's turn. If you hang onto the ball too long, the game falters. If you force the ball onto your partner too soon, the game is no longer any fun. If one kid ran up and grabbed the ball out of the other kid's hand, the game wouldn't work.

Conversation is like a game of *catch*. You get to talk only when the ball is tossed to you. If you grab the conversation out of the other person's hand, by interrupting, you ruin the game. Which leads to the woman's question, "When is it okay to interrupt?" (Thought I wouldn't get back to it, didn't you?) The answer is simple. Are you grabbing the ball out of someone's hand because you have something that is *extremely* interesting to add? If so, keep quiet and let your partner finish. Or are you interjecting in order to keep the flow going? If so, *good on you*. (I learned that compliment in Australia and never get to use it at home.)

An example was a conversation I had with a client. I was conducting a full-day workshop and the group took a lunch break. Some of the organizers were going to a nearby restaurant and one of the members offered to take me in his car. During the drive, I asked about how he got started in his position. He surprised me by saying that he didn't study for his profession, he actually attended college as a music major. My first thought was, "I wonder what instrument he played?" I really wanted to know what he played, but he had continued on, describing the interesting route he took from music to marketing. Even though I wanted to talk about his music studies, his intent for the conversation was to relate his fascinating journey from one career path to another. His intent was to fascinate me, so I needed to be fascinated.

What I did to maintain focus, which is difficult when you have an unanswered question burning in your mind, was to log my question about his instrument in the back of my mind, and listen to the rest of his story. I knew I could get back to my question at any time, but I couldn't let it inhibit my listening. And truthfully, if I never got back to my question, how much would it matter? In order to refocus on his story, I made sure to interject. I made sure my interjections connected to the intent of his story. When he finished, I got back around to my question. (By the way, he played saxophone.)

To develop the skills of listening and retention, we play an exercise in my workshops called *Five Minute Conversation*. Two people face each other. One person will speak and the other person will listen. The speaker must talk for five uninterrupted minutes. The speaker must talk about him/herself (not about the weather, sports, current events, or his or her work). This is an important rule because it is easy to deflect focus away from one's self by talking about unimportant chit-chat. Talking about one's self is what networking is all about. Even talking strictly about work is not allowed, because those who talk only about work make for lousy networking. Even if your business is interesting, if you aren't interesting as well, networking fails.

During the five-minute talk, the listener may not say a word. He or she may smile, nod, and look interested, but no talking! The speaker's goal is to keep the listener fully engaged. This means avoiding stalls like "Let's see. What else can I tell you about me?" or "I really don't have much else to say." It can be uncomfortable to be the focus of attention for five full minutes. And this type of conversation is unusual for people.

We are raised to communicate in a family/social environment. Conversations typically include verbal cues from the listener—"Oh really? What happened next?" or "You're kidding! What did she say?"—that help guide the conversation. Conversing without those cues can be unsettling. We build that challenge into *Five Minute Conversation* to help develop the skills of engaging the listener. The listener's job is a tough one. Keep your mouth shut. When the five minutes is up, however, then the listener speaks. She or he must now tell the speaker everything that was said. The goal should be to retell the story as verbatim as possible.

When we play this exercise, the reactions are two-fold. Some people have an incredibly difficult time talking about themselves for five straight minutes. They have likely honed their skills as listeners, and need to develop the ability to engage others in their story. Listening is an important skill, but unless you have something to say, you will be seen as the *friend who is a really good listener*. Remember those friends in high school? They never got a date. Others report that having to listen for five straight minutes was nearly impossible. They wanted to interrupt and ask more about a part of the story that interested them. Or they wanted to share a story of their own that connected to something the speaker said. These aren't negative urges, they just need to be controlled. Control begins by being conscious of one's motives.

You can play *Five Minute Conversation* without anyone being aware of it. The next time someone is telling you a story, see how long you can go without redirecting or interjecting your own experiences into the story. When someone is talking and you feel the urge to speak, ask yourself whether you are interjecting or interrupting. And whether you are being thrown the ball, or you are grabbing it from the other kid's hand.

Are you aware of the fact that we can see you?

I was at a workshop and I noticed a man and woman chatting after my session. The man was leaning slightly away from the woman and had his arms crossed over his chest. I asked him if he knew he was giving pretty strong *disinterested in what you are saying* signals. He said that he always crossed his arms because he had a sore back and the posture relieved pressure on his spine. I reminded him that, while the explanation makes perfect sense, because his partner didn't know about his bad back, she could easily have misinterpreted his signals. She said that, indeed, that was the case.

Remember Paul Sills, the founder and director of *The Second City* theatre in Chicago whom I spoke of earlier? He had a way of cutting through the bull and getting to the point. During one exercise at the week-long intensive I attended, one of the participants was completely *in his head* and performing without seeming to be aware of anyone else in the exercise. Some instructors would have commented, "Hey. You have to be aware of other people" but Sills stopped the exercise, walked up to the young man and said, "Are you aware of the fact that we can see you?" Comments like this may take a while to understand, but they make their point. And what connects his comment to networking is the importance of body language.

Before you rush out and buy a stack of books that analyze each movement and posture, know that the study of body language is as important as it is inexact. One person may fold their arms and legs in a display of distrust, while someone else does it because the room is cold. And quite often we negatively misinterpret the signals from others. During one of my workshops, a man sat in the front row with his arms tightly folded, with a scowl on his face. No matter how engaging or funny my presentation was, the rest of the audience would be laughing and nodding their heads while he sat stone-faced. It was the longest two hours of my life. After the workshop concluded, he approached me with a big smile and said, "That was great! I enjoyed every minute of it." I looked around to see if it was the same guy who had scowled at me for what seemed like eternity. I mentioned the encounter to a friend of mine who is a behavior expert. My friend said, "Oh. He is most likely an auditory learner."

My friend explained that, because the visual cortex is the largest and most efficient part of the brain for receiving and evaluating information, the majority of people are considered *visual learners*. In order to process input, visual learners need to see photos, graphs, and charts. However, there is a percentage of the population that is considered *auditory learners*. These people process through sound and words. In order for an auditory learner to concentrate, they will usually shut down other forms of input; physical, visual, etc. So the gentleman at my workshop folded his arms and closed down any movement in order to minimize distraction. The facial expression that I interpreted as an angry scowl was merely him concentrating on my words.

Psychologists also consider some people to be *kinesthetic learners*. In order to process sensory input, kinesthetic learners need to move, touch, and experience the physical world around them. *Olfactory learners* do best in environments that have a pleasing aroma. Certain scents calm them, so they light scented candles at home and use aroma kits in the car. *Guttural learners* like to munch on snacks. It isn't necessarily eating food that calms and focuses them, it is the process of eating. These folks will sit at a movie theatre with a box of popcorn, but instead of eating the popcorn and then watching the movie. They will eat one kernel at a time throughout the entire movie. With all this, you can see why trying to interpret someone's body language is, at best, an inexact science. If you get ten different body language experts in a room, you will get eleven different opinions. Be that as it may, there are at least some universal truths that we must all be aware of when being in the same physical space of other homo sapiens.

One universal truth is that you must be at least aware of how you physical/visually appear to others. And you must know if there is intent behind your physicality, or if you are moving, standing, or gesturing out of mindless habit. Focusing on the intent behind your actions is a good way to focus on your own behavior instead of trying to evaluate the body language of someone else. Being mindful of your own signals can help you avoid faux pas. For example, personal space.

Few things can drive a conversation partner crazier than not reading his or her signals meant to inform you of the appropriate distance to stand away from them. I was networking with a group of executives prior to my presentation. One man approached me, gave a good handshake, had a great smile and a genuine demeanor. Then he leaned in toward me, way in. Way, way in. Have you ever had a conversation with someone who invades your personal space, so you take a small step backward, only to have them take yet another step toward you? I kept backing away from this man and he kept moving forward until my back was against a wall. It didn't help that he would have seriously benefited from a box of Tic-Tacs.

The human brain is equipped with *mirror neurons*. These neurons are designed to cause people to imperceptibly adjust their posture and movements to match those around them. Humans who match those around them demonstrate social awareness and the ability to blend in with the group; an advantageous trait in an animal with an advanced brain. I wouldn't suggest blatantly mirroring the physicality of everyone around you, but be mindful of the cues being sent to you, and react accordingly.

One of these things is not like the other

Being a weak species on the planet, human survival has depended largely on our ability to work together; to depend on the social network to protect and advance each individual within the group. The evolutionary holdover of this fact is that humans value *similarity* above most other qualities. Put simply, people do not ponder their options and then decide what action to take. They do what other people who look like them, dress like them, and sound like them do. Mob mentality doesn't just exist during protests or raucous celebrations, it is a part of all of our DNA.

The urge to connect with other similar humans is so strong, it guides human reaction to others on a subconscious level. In a controlled study, subjects were asked to sit in a small booth in which the faces of various people were flashed on a screen. While the subjects looked at photos of faces, their immune response system was being continuously monitored. Whenever a face appeared that was from a different geographic region, the subject's immune system spiked. Likewise, when the *foreign* face was accompanied by a voice that had a different regional dialect than the subject, the immune system spiked again. Keep in mind, the face or voice being deemed foreign was based on geography. Facial features carry the mark of the owner's origin, so a face from Ireland has different features than a face from Poland, even though both faces could have the same skin color, they appear foreign to each other. And the number of dialects in the U.S. alone make America the land of many sub-cultures.

The spike in the auto-immune system in response to a dissimilar face or voice is because, throughout history, strangers have meant danger, but not necessarily because of armed conflict. Through the millennia, more people have died from germs and pathogens than from spears or arrows. As a result, and without so much as a quick heads-up to our conscious brain, our auto-immune system took over and developed responses to keep us alive. When the body detects an *other* in our presence, it prepares to defend itself from an unseen attack from germs. This might explain why racism is so difficult to erase. When we see someone who looks foreign, our subconscious is saying, "Danger!"

However, the auto-immune system is a part of the lower-brain system. The part of the brain that reacts with fear and panic, the amygdala, sits down there in the lower brain screaming "Yes!" "No!" "Want!" and "Don't want!" without much consideration for the outcome. That is a good thing because, if a bear starts chasing you or a person points a spear at you, you don't want the thinking part of the brain to ponder, "Boy, this doesn't feel right. I wonder what I should do now." You want your legs moving. The amygdala may have an impact on our conscious decision making, but it doesn't entirely control it. Once images and voices reach the prefrontal cortex, and thinking overcomes reacting, we realize that what seemed like vast differences between people are really just a mirage. And what differences do exist aren't really as dangerous as we first thought. In fact, these differences make life interesting. It is important, however, to discuss how all this affects networking.

Networking is a pretty big blast in the face for the poor little reactive amygdala. If you are at a crowded networking event, the amygdala has to quickly react to dozens of new faces and voices and decide *safe* or *unsafe*. Do you ever feel tired at the end of a night of networking? That is your brain working overtime. So a good networker will make things easy on the brain of the other person. You will send signals that tell the other amygdala that it can relax and go back to playing video games.

The best signal to send—the signal that erases all feelings of foreign-ness, that eases the immune system back to normal, that tells the amygdala everything is *safe*—is also the simplest tool we have. A human smile. A good smile is the quickest, and best, signal the brain can receive. And you would be surprised at how often I observe people at functions greet each other without a smile. Or worse, with a fake one. Flashing a fake smile is worse than no smile at all because it is a glaring signal to the other person that you are not to be trusted.

>"*Acting is all about honesty.*
>*If you can fake that, you've got it made.*"
>George Burns

What you want is a *Duchenne Smile*, named for the French neurologist who studied facial expressions. Duchenne discovered that a genuine smile involves contraction of both the *zygomatic major muscle* (which raises the corners of the mouth), and the *orbicularis oculi muscle* (which raises the cheeks and forms crow's feet around the eyes). A non-Duchenne smile only involves the mouth, the *zygomatic major muscle*. A smile that doesn't involve the whole face—the mouth, the eyes, and the cheeks—is not a smile at all. A non-Duchenne, or fake, smile is often called a *Pan Am* smile; referring to the old airline, Pan American. Pan American flight attendants were trained to smile at all passengers, but this often led to an insincere expression.

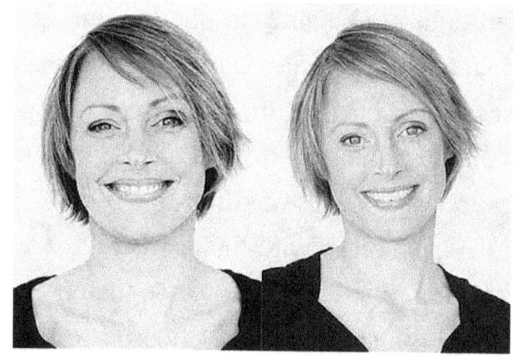

Pan American   Duchenne

Pan American   Duchenne

How do you get the *Duchenne* smile when the inside of your brain is saying "Get me out of here"? You develop an attitude where you are genuinely happy to meet new people. Let's discuss how you do that next.

I think I can, I think I can

If you don't recognize the title of this section, you have to go back and read the classic children's book, *The Little Engine That Could*. The story, first published in 1902 in a Swedish Journal, is a lesson for children about the importance of perseverance and optimism. There is some fascinating new research that brings to light just how powerful this kind of thinking is, and how you can use it to your advantage.

Whenever we engage in an activity is challenging, or where the outcome is both important and uncertain, humans engage in *self-talk*. It is nearly impossible for humans to undertake meaningful activities without silently talking to ourselves about the potential outcome. And the math is simple, the more impact the outcome will have on our lives, the greater the amount of self-talk we engage.

Self-talk is not simply talking our way through the activity, it is a means of prediction. The human brain loves to predict the outcome of every encounter, but it isn't happy with offering a prediction and seeing what happens. No, the brain likes to be *right* about its prediction. It wants its prediction to be right so badly that the brain will affect our behavior during the encounter in order to push us toward the outcome it predicted. If the prediction was that the encounter would fail, the brain will subtly sabotage our efforts to ensure failure. If the brain predicted a win, it will push in that direction. This is a process that psychologists call *psychological consistency*. The term refers to the fact that the brain likes its psychology, its thinking, to be consistent with behaviors and outcomes. Outcomes that are inconsistent with the brain's prediction cause discord. Discord is damaging; so much so that the brain would rather have a terrible outcome that matches its prediction, than a good outcome.

Psychological consistency dictates that, if you predict a negative outcome, the brain will work to ensure it happens. If you predict a positive outcome you will perform better, often without knowing why. The discovery of psychological consistency is what spawned the *self-affirmation* movement. Self-affirmations are the verbal positive statements one says to one's self in order to boost self-confidence and performance. Self-affirmations were the target of the *Saturday Night Live* character, Stuart Smalley, created by writer and comedian, Al Franken. Smalley's daily, "I'm good enough. I'm smart enough. And doggone it, people like me" affirmations were great comedic fodder, but there is sound research to affirm (get it?) their effectiveness. I mean, Franken went on to become a United States Senator for the State of Minnesota, so affirmations must do some good, right?

So, why talk about self-talk in a book about networking? Because networking has both qualities that can throw the brain into a spiral of poor performance: the outcome is important, and the outcome is uncertain. How many times have you walked into a roomful of strangers and thought, "What am I doing here? I'll just make the best of it, engage in some small talk and get the heck out of here." Or, when someone approached you and you thought, "Oh man. How long to I have to talk to this person before I can make an excuse to leave?" Because the power of self-talk is subconscious, you may not even be aware of how you are sabotaging the very efforts you are putting into networking. The good news is, you can make psychological consistency work for you instead of against you. It just takes conscious effort and discipline (which is why most people don't do it).

If done correctly, the self-affirmation version of self-talk has a marked impact on the brain. First, what-ever you say to yourself must be out loud. Simply thinking good thoughts does have some impact, but research has discovered that when the brain hears its own voice, it triggers the brain to better accept the message. Also, the self-talk must be repeated over a period of time. What self-talk is doing is rewriting the brain's internal script; rewiring set patterns of thinking. The longer a certain type of thinking has been in place, the more work it takes to rewire the circuits. So you need to repeat phrases a few times a day over the course of weeks, sometimes months, depending on the severity of the issue and how deep-seated the fear or negativism.

New research has uncovered an important tool that boosts the power of self-talk to an even higher level. It is the use of your own name instead of a personal pronoun. Using the personal pronouns "I" or "me" may actually cause you to become flustered, and perform poorly. However, if you say, "Stevie, you know you are going to do well tonight" your performance improves. Psychologist Ethan Kross was intrigued by the *name versus personal pronoun* effect after a number of occasions where he heard people refer to themselves in the third person instead of saying "I" or "me." After extensive research, Kross discovered that when people use a personal pronoun, different parts of the brain activate than when they use their own name.

Using one's own name toggles a switch in the brain so that the experience shifts away from the amygdala and into the cortex. This provides objectivity and self-distance, which aids in emotional control. Kross also discovered that using one's own name minimized *rumination*, which is when we relive experiences over and over after the fact, which increases anxiety and inhibits performance. In one experiment, Kross asked 89 men and women to give a speech (easily the most stressful act an adult can perform). Each participant was given five minutes to prepare. Half were instructed to use only pronouns to describe themselves in a preparatory document; the other half were told to use their given name. Those in the pronoun group experienced anxiety and reported viewing the task as impossible. A typical response was, "How can I possibly write a speech in five minutes?" Those who used their names felt less anxiety approaching the task and felt highly confident. "You can do it, Ethan," was a typical phrase in the run-up to a speech.

But the real test came afterward. Those using their name performed better on the speech (judged by independent evaluators) and engaged in far less rumination afterward; they also experienced less depression and felt less shame. "When dealing with strong emotions, taking a step back and becoming a detached observer can help," Kross explains. "It's very easy for people to advise their friends, yet when it comes to themselves, they have trouble. But people engaging in this process, using their own first name, are distancing themselves from the self, right in the moment, and that helps them perform."

Using one's name also eases the workload of the brain. Jason Moser, a neuroscientist and clinical psychologist at Michigan State University measured electrical activity in the brain as subjects engaged in different varieties of self-talk. Moser showed two groups of women photographs of a masked man holding a knife to a woman's throat. One group of women was prone to chronic worrying, the other was psychologically normal. Each group was then asked to elaborate about a positive outcome through self-talk while Moser measured electrical activity in the lobes of the frontal cortex and in the limbic system.

When women used the pronouns *I* and *me* in their self-talk, worriers had to work much harder than non-worriers to talk themselves into a positive view—and even then they failed to calm themselves down. They dwelled on fears that the woman under attack had died. The harder their frontal lobes worked, the more anxious their limbic brain became;

the task pitched them into a vicious circle of rumination, anxiety, and more rumination.

The same women were asked to repeat the self-talk exercise, only this time deliberately using their first names instead of personal pronouns. They reported a dramatic reduction in anxiety levels. Electrodes picked up the psychic improvement by documenting a vast reduction in energy consumed by the frontal lobes. What's more, the frantic cries of the amygdala quieted down as well, its activity reduced by just about half.

In order for self-talk to correctly position psychological consistency to your advantage, you must include three important steps. Take a look at the statement below.

"Becky (1), what are you nervous about? This isn't the first time you have been in a room with people you don't know. I know you want to do well, but don't put the weight of your company on your shoulders (2), and stay calm. Even if it doesn't go perfectly, it won't be the end of the world. You are capable (3), intelligent, and accomplished. Just do your best. Get in there and have fun, Becky."

1) Becky distances herself from the stress of networking by addressing herself by name, seeing herself as she would a friend. The distance confers wisdom, confidence, and calm she would never have if she used *I* or *me*.

2) She uses the kinds of strategies children use when engaging in activities like building with blocks, only instead of instructing herself to put the small square on top of the big

rectangle, she now tells herself to be calm. Her self-direction is precise.

3) Finally, Becky alleviates the gravity of the situation with a few self-affirmations, allowing her to see the situation in the context of her whole being. She will not be devastated or ruminate endlessly on the experience if she doesn't connect with a million dollar client.

In order to use self-talk effectively, you cannot simply recognize that you feel anxiety, you have to know the specific cause of your anxiety. I used the power of self-talk to rewrite the psychological consistency I experienced at a workshop. In my case, anxiety is caused, not by the make-up of the audience, but by their attitude about being there. I don't particularly like sessions with mandatory attendance. Because my goal is to teach new skills, it works best if people actually want to learn.

One day I got a call from the Department of Corrections. They asked if I could conduct a workshop dealing with team work. If corrections officers in prisons don't work smoothly with teammates, real danger can result. The workshop was to take place in the gymnasium at a state prison (nothing like a sunny, happy place to conduct a teamwork session). When I arrived, the director of training met me at the front gate and escorted me down the long hallway to the gym. While we walked, she hit me with a bombshell, "This workshop isn't for the entire corrections staff, it is only for the prison guards. They hate these workshops. Union regulations require that we have two professional development workshops a year, and they hate being here on their day off. There is a guy talking about retirement benefits and then you're on." She finished with, "Have fun!"

Have fun? Was she serious? I peeked around the corner and saw 250 burly guys who could either be at home (remember, this is their day off), or with me learning about teamwork. When I said I felt anxiety about workshops with mandatory attendance, I forgot to include audiences that are heavily armed. The worst part was I was to work with this group, and come back the next day to work with the other half of the prison guard staff. So if these guys didn't like me, the other guys would hear about it. I looked around at the prison cells surrounding the gym and wondered if any of them were reserved for me, just in case my workshop tanked.

My mind was spinning, but I knew I had a job to do. So I put the psychological consistency effect to the test. While the presenter was finishing with his talk about retirement, I stepped into a private room and said, "Come on, Stevie. Calm down. You know you are only freaking out because she said they hate these workshops, but they look like a great bunch of guys. They haven't had one of *your* workshops, and they are going to love it. They look like they want to have fun. So you're going to go out there, own that stage, and have a great time. Own it, Stevie!"

It is important to note that psychological consistency and self-talk are subconscious processes. Your conscious brain is still very much awake during your self-talk, and it quite often tells you you're crazy. The entire time I was speaking self-affirmations, my conscious brain was saying, "Are you nuts? How can you say they look like fun guys when they look like they want to dig their own tunnel out of this prison?" And, because the conscious brain relies on memory, mine was saying, "This kind of audience has never worked well in the past. This is going to suck!" This is why self-talk is so important. You must overcome the fear and anxiety of your conscious brain, no matter how accurately you think it is reading the situation.

The result was, it was one of the best workshops I have ever had. The guys were actually anxious to learn, and to have fun doing it. They were just tired of the same old PowerPoint speeches they were subjected to over the years. As you might guess, prison guards are people of action, so they don't take to sitting for long periods of time while someone lectures at them. So I made the session active. I also used their style of humor to connect with them. You can guess that the type of humor in a prison is quite different than at an elementary school. Humor bonds people, and prison guards use good natured jabs at each other to build cohesive teams. So I used the same style of humor, gesturing to one guard in the audience and saying, "Good to see you here, sir. By the way, the '50s called and they want their haircut back." When the audience howled with laughter, it wasn't because the joke was hilarious, it was because "Stevie picked on Charlie!" Then I looked at another guy and asked, "Are you married?" When he said, "Yes" I responded, "I could tell, because no single guy would wear that shirt." More howls, with guys smacking him on the arm. I returned the next day to conduct the workshop for the other half of the staff. Four guards met me at the front gate with, "Are you going to pick on guys like you did yesterday?" I said, "Probably." They smiled, pulled out a piece of paper and said, "Great. We've got some names for you."

Examine your self-talk before you walk in the door. If it is negative, go off on your own and turn it around. Take a tip from me, do this in a private room. You don't need 250 prison guards staring at you.

CHAPTER 8

Making It Work

Creativity is borne of structure. You can't be in the moment and create if you don't have a solid foundation. A good example of how structure fosters creativity is the world of music. Music has existed for centuries, but has foundered for most of its early history. Early music was created largely by chance—someone discovering that a piece of metal made a sound when struck against a log, or a tone was produced by blowing over the lid of a jar—but, these discoveries didn't grow beyond their simple beginnings. All that changed with the creation of a simple structure, the eight-note octave scale. When the scale "Do Re Mi Fa Sol La Ti Do" was invented, music was given something it never had before; structure. The new structure allowed musicians to codify their creations; and to record them so the music could proliferate. Rather than inhibit creativity, as some assume occurs with structure, it caused an explosion of music worldwide.

Networking is a highly creative endeavor. Those who approach it as simply a process are rarely successful (like Susie Jamison, our super-networker from Chapter One).

Adding structure to the creative process of networking will allow you to flourish. The games and exercises discussed so far are a good start. Actually practicing them on a regular basis would be even better. To that end, here is more helpful structure.

Set Goals. No one would be foolish enough to start a business without clear goals, however people walk into a networking function without a clue as to what they specifically want to achieve. They wait until the end of the event to decide whether it was worth their time. Imagine starting a business and waiting until you are bankrupt to decide if things are going alright.

Set a goal before each networking function; meet five new people, create one good business connection, focus on your partner and don't talk about yourself too much, or don't leave until you have one person so intrigued that they ask for your business card. You may alter your goal if a better opportunity arises, but you are not allowed to weasel out of your goal simply because you are uncomfortable.

Get a Networking Buddy. Goals are much easier to achieve if you share them with someone. Have a friend attend the event with you. The purpose of this networking buddy is two-fold; 1) you now have someone with whom to share your goals, 2) you have someone to whom you are accountable. Another benefit of a networking buddy is to have someone to check in with during the event. Having a support person makes networking a lot easier. If your networking buddy can't attend the event, ask a friend or colleague to be available later so you can check in after the function. This person's purpose is to hold you accountable to your goals. If you didn't meet your original goal because you were busy accomplishing an even better goal, your networking buddy gives you a pat on the back, but if you didn't meet your goal because you simply backed out, it is good to have someone who can create a plan to help you do better next time. The final benefit of a networking buddy is that if you are stuck talking to someone you can't get away from, you can call your buddy over, introduce the two, and slip away, leaving your buddy stuck. I did that to Gary once. It was great fun.

Own Your Space. The old advice that you only have thirty seconds to make a good impression is not quite true. You do have about thirty seconds to really connect once a conversation has started, but the impressions we make are created when we first enter the room. The next time you are at a professional or social gathering, take a moment and examine the other networkers. See who looks comfortable. See who looks like they are waiting for someone else to make them comfortable.

In my training as a martial artist I was taught to *own my space*. Owning your space means that you are in control of your surroundings. You exude a confidence that shows that others can relax around you. Owning your space means that you don't try to dominate others, yet you will not shy away from them. Give others the feeling that this is your space and you have complete control over it. This control is not meant to subjugate others, but to serve them and make them feel comfortable. This is not the kind of control in which you dictate what is to occur, but that you are flexible to whatever happens.

When I am preparing for a presentation, I prepare to *own the space* by arriving early. With no one else in the room, I walk around and become familiar with my surroundings. This makes an incredible difference when it comes time for me to speak. You can accomplish this without arriving early. During an event, take a moment to step back and look over the room. Don't just observe the goings-on, observe the space as if it was yours. Doing this changes your perspective. Instead of being acted upon by your surroundings and the people in it, you take control. Even if you aren't the host of the event, everyone suddenly become *your* guest.

Say, "Next." It isn't likely that you will be totally rejected while networking, but it does happen. What then? A great business coach of mine once said, "If they say 'No,' you say 'Next!'" Good sales professionals actually love hearing the word "No." It means they can stop wasting everyone's time and move on to another prospect. They don't take "no" as a personal rejection, because it rarely is. They take it as reality; not everyone will, or should, want what you offer. If you are networking correctly and focusing on the other person's needs, you should meet with success. Don't stew about it, say, "Next!"

A Final Word

A business coach once told me, "Don't let the chance of past success dictate future behavior." If things go well, we can't expect momentum to carry forward. And, if we fail, we cannot simply hope for the best next time. Make practicing networking skills a game, not a chore. Every time you go to the store, the bank, or any place you encounter a stranger, initiate a short conversation. Don't let transactional interactions take control of themselves. You take control and guide the interaction. You would never wait until the day of a presentation to break out your notes and take a look-see. Don't wait until a networking event is upon you to start thinking of how you might work the room. To do that is the same as practicing in front of the client. We would certainly think it foolish for an Olympic athlete to practice on the day of the event. To practice networking skills during the event is just as foolish.

Remember, whoever you meet will either be nervous or comfortable depending on your behavior. Put those around you at ease by taking care of them. Remember that, in order to take care of others you must first take care of yourself. Don't judge yourself too harshly, be yourself, and have fun.

I hope this book helps you gain more business, achieve higher goals, and have a little more fun the next time a networking opportunity arises. If we run across each other at a function in the future, I look forward to getting your business card. Just make sure I ask for it first!

Now, go work the room.

About the Author

Stephen "Stevie Ray" Rentfrow was born a small boy, which worked out so well he decided to remain one. Stevie co-founded *Stevie Ray's Improv Company* in 1989 and continues to run it with his partner, Pamela Mayne. He is a nationally syndicated columnist for the Business Journal Newspapers, a corporate trainer, and keynote speaker.

Stevie Ray is the only person in the country to design his own college degree, *Theory and Performance of Comedy* (his parents were *so* proud). He has he toured the country performing with such stars as "Weird Al" Yankovic, Paula Poundstone, Marsha Warfield of *Night Court,* and Rich Hall of *Saturday Night Live*. He is a lot funnier on stage than he is in this book.

A martial artist since 1977, he has studied seven martial arts and holds four black belts in four of them. At one point in his career he was a bodyguard for Pee Wee Herman (yes, really).

Stevie is also a beekeeper and producer of *Steve's Bees Minnesota Honey* and a volunteer for the Minnesota State Services for the Blind, recording books on tape for the blind.

Stevie lives in Minneapolis with his wife, Kanitta and stepdaughter, Ondine.

Other books by Stevie Ray

About the Rent
One Thousand Punches a Day
Quick Thinking for Any Situation
Speaking in Public without Sweating in Private
Spontaneity Takes Practice
The Birth, Life, (and sometimes death), of a Comedian
The Calm Before the Brainstorm
Three Big Words
What We Laugh At... and Why